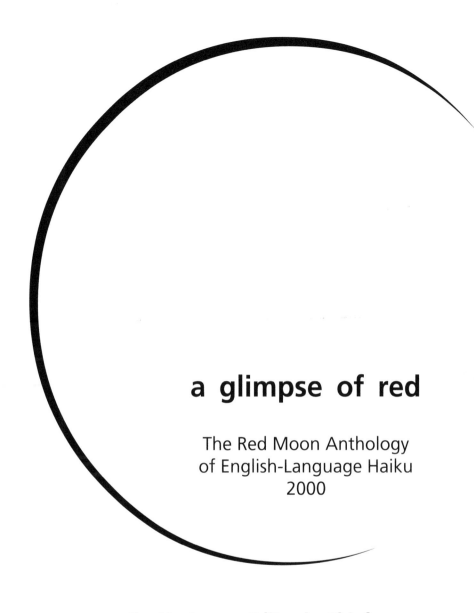

a glimpse of red

The Red Moon Anthology
of English-Language Haiku
2000

Jim Kacian ✧ **Editor-in-Chief**

Dimitar Anakiev ✧ **Jan Bostok**
Tom Clausen ✧ **Ellen Compton** ✧ **Dee Evetts**
Maureen Gorman ✧ **Kohjin Sakamoto**
Alan Summers ✧ **George Swede** ✧ **Jeff Witkin**

Published by
Red Moon Press
P. O. Box 2461
Winchester VA
22604-1661 USA
redmoon@shentel.net

ISBN 1-893959-18-X

Special thanks to
Neca Stoller and A. C. Missias for help
in the preparation of this volume.

Cover painting: *Izmak*
Branko Nikolov, 2000: litho print.
Privately owned. Used by permission.

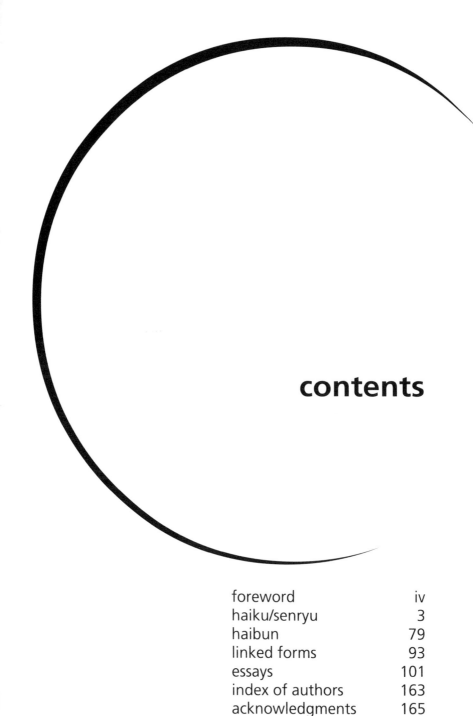

contents

foreword

THE RED MOON ANTHOLOGY of English-Language Haiku celebrates, with this volume, its fifth anniversary of publication. During this very fast half-decade we have had the pleasure to publish the very best work of hundreds of excellent poets. Moreover, the publication of the Red Moon Anthology has become a part of the haiku community's seasonal cycle: an eagerly anticipated event. And inclusion in the volume is a recognized reward.

This is a very gratifying development to all of us who toil at this time-consuming and finicky job. None of this could be accomplished, of course, without a staff of generous and dedicated editors, who read, nominate, vote and select the work which is gathered together in each RMA. It is worth noting again that they do this despite the fact that it actually puts them at a disadvantage to appear within the covers of the books themselves. A poet's work requires at least a 50% acceptance rate (5 or more votes from the 10 members of the editorial staff) in order to be included; but an RMA editor's task is much more difficult. An editor may not vote for his or her own work, and so must receive 5 votes from the other 9 editors, or 55%. In addition, an editor may nominate anyone's work—except his own. So it is harder for an editor's work to be nominated, and once nominated, harder for that work to be accepted, into the pages of RMA.

Of course, the editors of RMA are amongst the best practitioners of haiku in the world, and so they manage to be represented despite the odds against them, along with the many others whose work merits such attention. All of which makes RMA the best single source to discover the best of what is being written in contemporary haiku. It is my pleasure to share yet another volume of this award-winning series with you. Enjoy!

Jim Kacian
Editor-in-Chief

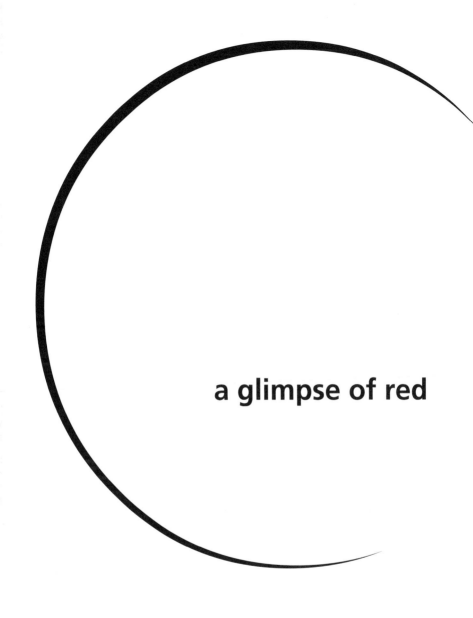

a glimpse of red

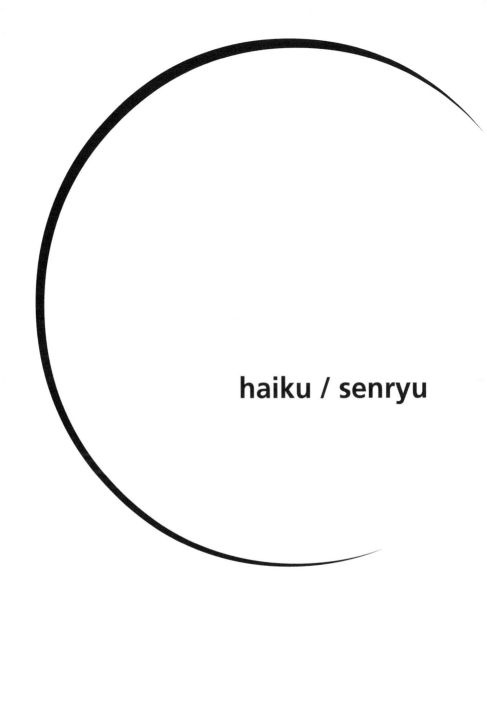

haiku / senryu

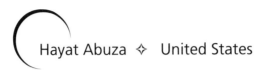

Hayat Abuza ✧ United States

heat wave
a taste of rain blown in
by the fan

Stephen Addiss ✧ United States

birthday snow
stepping into holes
left by the postman

an'ya ✧ United States

night of stars
all along the precipice
goat bells ring

Dimitar Anakiev ✧ Slovenia

cowbell—
the first sun arrives
in the village

Fay Aoyagi ✧ United States

> pre-surgery dinner
> tiny ocean
> in the oyster shell

John Bird ✧ Australia

> spring rain—
> each empty swing hangs
> above its puddle

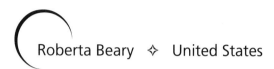

Roberta Beary ✧ United States

waiting room
the ex-wife looks
past me

all day long
I feel its weight
the unworn necklace

custody hearing
seeing his arms cross
I uncross mine

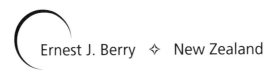

Ernest J. Berry ✧ New Zealand

old garden shed
the insecticide can
full of spiders

no-man's land
the rattle of a troop train
returning empty

Mykel Board ✧ United States

safe for a while
around the haiku poets
the fly

John Brandi ✧ United States

Fallen leaves—
the abbot sweeps
around them

Robert Boldman ✧ United States

the mourners gone
the church pews
refill with light

sultry night:
a corpse extracted
from the tenement

Randy Brooks ✧ United States

mountain butterfly
from her boulder
to mine

Kevin Brophy ✧ Australia

out of kindness now
I shout at my father
going deaf

Greba Brydges-Jones ✧ New Zealand

my forgetfulness
now reminding me
of my mother

Karen Buckley ✧ Wales

Behind the hearse
the rubbish lorry
keeps its distance

Alexius Burgess ✦ United States

hip fracture—
grapevine slowly encircles
the house

Michael Cadnum ✧ United States

By sunset
still no snow
my letter to you blank

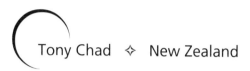

Tony Chad ✦ New Zealand

in the dark hallway—
avoiding the old black dog
years after he's gone

Yu Chang ✦ United States

new in town
the scent
of unknown flowers

Cyril Childs ✧ New Zealand

psychology exam—
one of the students
out-stares me

my wife's breast—
the surgeon gauges
my reaction

first chemo—
the waiting-room eyes
size us up

Pamela Connor ✦ United States

old broom . . .
still in the shape
of its sweep

John Crook ✦ England

summer solstice
the sun reaches a new place
on the fridge

Anne LB Davidson ✧ United States

rain on the skylight
putting on my red sweater
to peel potatoes

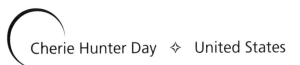

Cherie Hunter Day ✧ United States

a salamander
passing the coolness
hand to hand

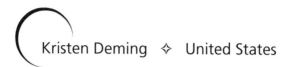

Kristen Deming ✧ United States

a leaf falls—
the column of gnats
reassembles

breaking the silence
of the drought
acorn rain

one year becomes another—
snow disappearing
into snow

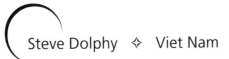

Zoran Doderovic ✧ Yugoslavia

Fallen magnolia petals;
The little girl makes
a new flower

Steve Dolphy ✧ Viet Nam

on a park bench
the old couple
feeding separate pigeons

Patricia Donegan ✧ Japan

> pampas grass
> bending—
> endless dreams

Fred Donovan ✧ United States

> watching the girl
> in a short tight skirt
> I fondle my pocket change

Del Doughty ✧ United States

peeing after sex—
outside cars slosh
through melting snow

John J. Dunphy ✧ United States

All Souls Day
my neighbor cleans
his hunting rifle

Peter Duppenthaler ✧ Japan

into twilight
colors you cannot name
the evening bell

Dennis H. Dutton ✧ United States

the stillness when rain
drumming on the roof
turns to snow

Marlene J. Egger ✧ United States

sudden downpour
the waiter brings
another pot of coffee

Marikay Eldridge ✧ United States

ebb tide
every footprint leaves
another moon

Judson Evans ✧ United States

summer thunder
slow knit of bone
beneath the cast

Michael L. Evans ✧ United States

midnight snow
my thoughts drift
to the white chessmen

Dee Evetts ✧ United States

deep in the mountains
the shaving mirror
shows me the mountains

Michael Fessler ✧ Japan

beating a rug
the solution
comes to me

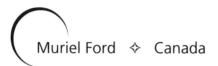

Muriel Ford ✧ Canada

rainy afternoon . . .
watching fractals
blossoming

Stanford M. Forrester ✧ United States

temple bell ringing
one thousand times . . .
winter rain

Marco Fraticelli ✧ Canada

last night of holidays
I whisper secrets
to my sleeping wife

Jack Galmitz ✧ United States

Behind the wide load
The traffic comes to a halt—
The green mountains

D. Claire Gallagher ✧ United States

winter drizzle
popping corn rattles
the dented lid

the closer we get . . .
losing my friend's heart to heart
to the waterfall

winking
the bride promises
to obey

Barry George ✧ United States

Winter morning—
the sound of a board
hitting the pile

Joyce Austin Gilbert ✧ United States

leftover drumsticks
. . . first Christmas
without dad

Robert Gilliland ✧ United States

morning glory
gently the postman
opens the gate

Penelope Greenwell ✧ United States

geese in flight—
the untidy stitches
of her last quilt

31

LeRoy Gorman ✧ Canada

in a field I knew
my son digs
for fossils

a child's
headstone
breaks
the blossom
fall

her clingy skirt
the static
between us

Lee Gurga ✧ United States

what to do?
a penny face up
in the urinal

Carolyn Hall ✧ United States

fluttering faster
than I can riffle pages
in the fieldguide

Yvonne Hardenbrook ✧ United States

mountain hike
we drink from the beginning
of a great river

the clerk's lip ring—
I forget what
I wanted

Peggy Heinrich ✧ United States

> end of summer
> the shape of his feet
> in his sneakers

Claire Bugler Hewitt ✧ England

> solar eclipse
> and at the darkest point
> you call my name

Christopher Herold ✧ United States

foghorns . . .
we lower a kayak
into the sound

just a trickle
seeping between river stones
summer twilight

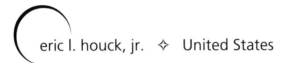

eric l. houck, jr. ✧ United States

breakfast
a chair left empty
fills with morning sun

Thomas Hoyt ✧ United States

drawing the bow
with perfect concentration . . .
panty lines

June Hopper Hymas ✧ United States

from hand to hand
the restroom key
—February rain

Ken Jones ✧ Wales

Well-thumbed public map
"You are here"
no longer there

Jim Kacian ✧ United States

undressing in the dark—
the sparks
from her sweater

reading the time travel novel into the next day

in concert
the solo violinist
and his shadows

Alain Kervern ✧ France

Coiled
in the rowers' hearts
the current's force.

Jerry Kilbride ✧ United States

condolence letter—
running out of ink
in mid-sentence

Michael Ketchek ✧ United States

gentle snow
the woodpile
still crooked

late snow
the faintest green tinge
in the honeysuckle

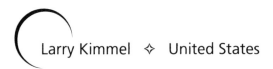

Larry Kimmel ✧ United States

surprise visit
I bury the hatchet
in the chopping block

Joann Klontz ✧ United States

overcast
I bother the blackbirds
for a glimpse of red

Rich Krivcher ✧ United States

train whistle—
river ice cracking
beneath the trestle

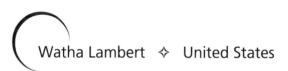

Watha Lambert ✧ United States

Bottles click—
the milkman delivers
another day.

Jack Lent ✧ United States

spring grass:
new graves blending
with the old

Martin Lucas ✧ England

new millennium
the lights on the bridge
curving into mist

Peggy Willis Lyles ✧ United States

into the night
we talk of human cloning
snowflakes

Catherine Mair ✧ New Zealand

night fishing
his line catching only
phosphorescence

Robert Major ✧ United States

Adjoining beds . . .
old golfers
comparing strokes

Makiko ✧ United States

snake hunting the boy sheds his shirt

Mami Matsuzaki ✧ Japan

first ice over the pond
colors of the morning
sealed inside

Michael McClintock ✧ United States

that kid
who stole my marbles,
buried today

Paul David Mena ✧ United States

> starless night
>   my children forget
>   to wave goodbye

Bogoljub Mihajovic ✧ Yugoslavia

> After the rain—
> barefoot children
> walking on the sky

Sue Mill ✧ Australia

cold rain—
the scent of peaches
fills the room

Emiko Miyashita ✧ Japan

I sink a little bridge
to the aquarium floor—
first day of summer

A. C. Missias ✧ United States

spring morning—
checking my fit
in the park swing

thinking about a man
I know is 'taken' . . .
three-quarter moon

Barry Morrall ✧ New Zealand

> dark river—
> one ripple going upstream
> against the current

Akiko Nakata ✧ Japan

> New rice is boiled.
> I offer a quantity
> To my dead parents

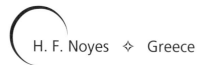

Pamela Miller Ness ✧ United States

    winter dawn
    emptying the wastebaskets
    after he leaves

H. F. Noyes ✧ Greece

    spring morning—
    the old dog lifts his leg
    a little higher

Sean O'Connor ✧ Ireland

4 a.m.
a neighbour I have never seen
watching the eclipse.

Marian Olson ✧ United States

Full moon—
I iron a wrinkle
into his pants

W. F. Owen ✧ United States

pet store
nose prints
both sides

flea market—
seeing my old shirt
on her new husband

lifting the hammer
the old carpenter's hand
stops shaking

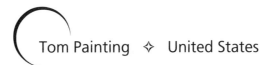

Tom Painting ✧ United States

a dry leaf
scratches along the sidewalk
All Souls' Day

James Paulson ✧ United States

bedtime story
the smell of leaves
in my daughter's hair

Aleksandar Pavic ✧ Yugoslavia

going nowhere
during the air-raid alarm—
a scarecrow

Kenneth Payne ✧ United States

fireflies—
remembering things
I've only imagined

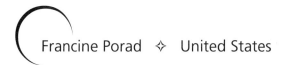

Francine Porad ✧ United States

long night
I adjust my breathing
to his

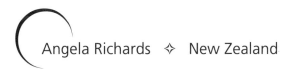

Angela Richards ✧ New Zealand

at the end of the garden
my mother
becomes flowers

David Rollins ✧ United Kingdom

this long journey
letting the wasp off
at Leeds

Charles Scanzello ✧ United States

tonight's lecture
on reincarnation . . .
I've heard it all before

Carla Sari ✧ Australia

airport strike
taking up smoking again
with a stranger

a waning moon the night train gathers speed

on the wrong platform
a new train
of thought

Daniel Schwerin ✦ United States

The mortician
    parks in my space—
        autumn evening

Eugina Shelton ✦ United States

creaking pew—
my tattoos hidden
by bandaids

Ernest Sherman ✧ United States

lilacs by the bridge—
soldier after soldier
catching the scent

Yasuhiko Shigemoto ✧ Japan

firefly—
its smell on the tip
of my finger

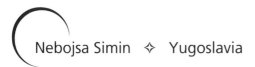

Nebojsa Simin ✦ Yugoslavia

Waiting
For another Bomb
sound of our breathing

Alan Spence ✦ Scotland

country road
too dark to see the flowers
but their scent is yellow

62

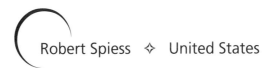 Robert Spiess ✧ United States

the pines on shore sway—
a mallard hen and ducklings
crest another wave

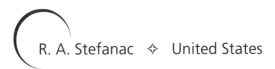 R. A. Stefanac ✧ United States

gingko biloba
forgetting where
I put it

Gary Steinberg ✧ United States

cemetery wind the cellophane of dead flowers crinkles

Celia Stuart-Powles ✧ United States

winter solstice
the glint of beaded mist
on the sweat lodge

John Stevenson ✧ United States

early Alzheimer's
she says she'll have . . .
the usual

snow
accumulating
traffic

homeless man—
the authorities seeking
the cause of death

George Swede ✧ Canada

intensive care
the shadows of falling leaves
on the sunlight wall

Brett Taylor ✧ United States

abandoned cabin
the sound of a pond loon
through broken glass

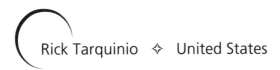

Rick Tarquinio ✦ United States

sectioned oak—
a daddy-long-legs spans
a dozen summers

chest to chest
the baby's heartbeat
between mine

winter night
spark of the house key
finding the lock

 Maurice Tasnier ✧ England

standing up
for a closer look
at the stars

pledging eternal love
she checks her watch

lengthening winter
    the white emptiness
    of the hospital bath

Marc Thompson ✧ United States

house guests—
putting the plain white sheets
on our bed

Tom Tico ✧ United States

autumn evening . . .
a page of the old book
separates from the spine

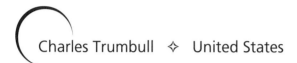

Charles Trumbull ✧ United States

click of the shutter
the whole family
exhales together

Cor van den Heuvel ✧ United States

city street
the darkness inside
the snow-covered cars

Zinovy Vayman ✧ Russia

fortress wall—
a pigeon sleeps in a hole
made by the shellfire

Max Verhart ✧ Netherlands

tin soldiers
the dead and the living
in the same box

Arnold Vermeeren ✧ Netherlands

storm clouds gather
an ant runs the edge
of the round table

Martin Vest ✧ United States

thoughts of youth—
a ceiling fan spins
in a teaspoon

Richard von Sturmer ✧ United States

each day less light,
the smell of printer's ink
on the morning newspaper

Paul Watsky ✧ United States

cafeteria—
watching their pastrami sliced
the hospital staff

Michael Dylan Welch   ✧   United States

meteor shower—
a gentle wave
wets our sandals

Valentine's Day—
she reminds me
to fasten my seatbelt

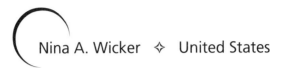

Nina A. Wicker ✧ United States

rain and more rain
ripping off the month
two days early

Vitomir Mletic Witata ✧ Yugoslavia

A hot barrel
of antiaircraft gun.
Spring rain evaporating.

Jeff Witkin ✧ United States

twilight . . .
a sailboat at anchor
turns with the tide

another ballgame
he brings her a sausage
too large for its bun

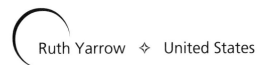

Ruth Yarrow ✧ United States

backstroke
under cirrus clouds—
flow of my fingertips

Edward Zuk ✧ Canada

The Milky Way—
one by one the children
light their sparklers

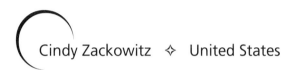

Cindy Zackowitz ✧ United States

north wind—
a cloud follows the valley
to the sea

scattered thoughts
along the trail—
this pocket full of keys

fresh snow
the last of the milk
saved for morning tea

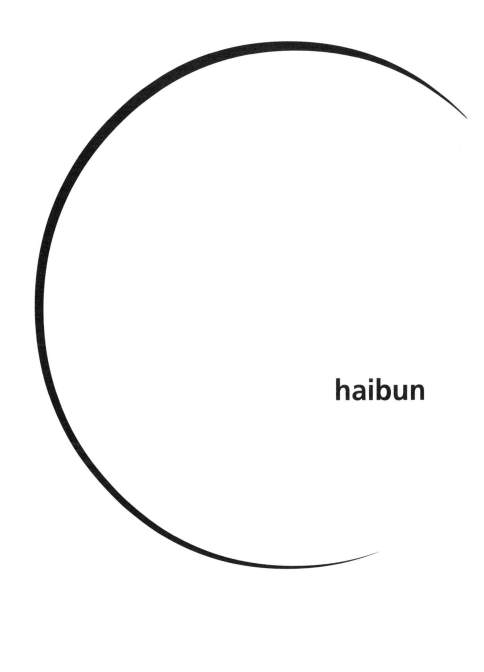

haibun

Yu Chang ✧ United States

Rain

Many people complain about the rain this spring, but the rain has always reminded me of when I was a young child growing up in a small village near Chungking, the wartime capital of China. A rainy day meant there was no need to run to the makeshift air-raid shelter, an old coal mine just beyond the terraced fields of the village. The grassy trails to the shelter could be quite slippery even when dry. One time, after the siren sounded, I ran so fast to try to catch up with everybody else that I fell face down into the field below. Oblivious to the mud all over my body, my mother hugged me after she pulled me up from the rice paddy. I wish now that I had said "I love you," but I just squirmed out of her arms. We were the last ones to get to the shelter. "We are safe now," she smiled.

> deep in the coal mine
> my mother's grip
> tightens

Dennis H. Dutton ✧ United States

The Bottom Line

On Dragon Mountain, we were cut off for weeks. When our food and water ran low, they choppered them in. It took that long to mop up the area and make it safe for truck and jeep traffic.

> Dragon Mountain
> at night on the bunker
> watching stars and tracers

One afternoon, at twilight, I saw just how costly the war was, and why we would eventually lose it. What I saw was one man in black pajamas running on the levee of a rice paddy, so far below that he looked like an ant. He was running hard, and with reason—a Huey helicopter gunship was shooting at him.

Once, he stopped. I think he must have been hit, but he didn't fall. Then he kept going, trying to make a copse of trees. The gunship fired without letup.

He almost made those trees.

Almost.

> black pajamas
> falling in the paddy
> all I can see from here

82

How much did it cost in dollars to kill that one man? Too much. How much in honor? Too much. It might have been from this time that I remember this image:

> shaving in my helmet
> someone else's face
> in the mirror

I don't know. I do know that I had changed, though not nearly as much as some:

> squad leader
> in each pocket for luck
> a shriveled ear

Dee Evetts ✧ United States

Potatoes

week of depression
draped on the bath tub
hand-washed socks

Alone in our apartment, I decide to call my mother in England to find out how she is. Suddenly it feels important to know that she is all right.

A little out of breath, she tells me her life is somewhat difficult right now, but she is planting her garden nonetheless, between showers. She describes this for me: spinach, onions, chard, even potatoes. "Not a real crop, I don't have room for that here. It may sound silly, but I still want to have the potato experience, so I'm planting just five." At these words, this image, I begin inexplicably to weep.

Unwilling to disturb the equilibrium at this moment, I tell her goodbye as soon as I can manage. Moving the short distance from my desk to the wingback chair by the window, I kneed backwards on it, looking at the sky. Through easy-flowing tears, I watch as a mourning dove lands just three feet away on the fire escape. It perches on one of our neglected windowboxes, and then settles down comfortably between two dead geraniums. This sight seems both to ease and prolong my crying, which finally ebbs away into a boundless sense of peace. For maybe half an hour I remain perfectly still, and so does the bird, except for an occasional movement of its filmy eyelids.

Later that day I am impelled to climb out onto the fire escape and pull up the dead plants, crumbling the packed soil with my fingers until it is loose and aerated again.

back from her trip
my wife with a tray
of geraniums

Patrick Frank ✧ United States

Haibun

Sleepless night in my single room I head for the coffee shop on foot my body feels cool the stars are blazing from the distant highway the hum of tractor trailers downshifting now upshifting.

I am alone but near to a special place there is a pathway through the woods leading to the railroad tracks I think of a woman who is far away she may never come back I am not angry wish she could explain

planet close to a sliver of the moon

I walk to the coffee shop at dawn I watch a brown sparrow dragging a stick then trying to fly but not giving up she has a brave heart it is beating in her chest she will not give up

spring morn bird's cry unceasing

Jerry Kilbride   ✧   United States

Losing Private Sutherland

Steven Spielberg's searing indictment of war—the bloody and horrendous carnage at Normandy Beach—was difficult to watch as I sat in the dark theater during a weekday matinee. Then, unexpectedly, the 506th was mentioned and I found myself on the verge of breaking down; that number identifying our basic training regiment triggered the old and unassuaged grief at Sutherland's death. A magnificent human being wasted in a forgotten war; the youth and promise of a good friend forfeited. I can still see him standing in combat boots smudged with Kentucky mud ... a residue of cold rain dripping from his helmet and poncho ... a cigarette in his mouth that he lights for me ... and then another he lights for himself. Pentimentoed under this memory, carried for almost 50 years, is a body riddled with bullets as it is washed away in the flashing rampage of a Korean river, and there follows a scene long and relentlessly willed to stave off madness ... *sediment settles gently on my friend's handsome face ... peacefully ... softly ... quietly* .... Yes, the soldier can no longer hear gunfire; the young soldier can no longer hear the river thundering into his throat. He is quiet ... as I soon will be quiet ...

the flag folded
something of myself is lowered
with his coffin

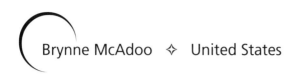

Brynne McAdoo ✧ United States

Breastless

I sit at my piano, cramming for my lesson, but can't focus. I think of my boyfriend, Tom, and his idea about how I can look "better."

"Honey, I'll pay for you to have a breast augmentation," he'd said, almost desperately. It was the same day he'd surprised me with flowers—probably to soften his proposal.

Now his flowers wilt in a vase on top of the piano. As I bang the keys and sing in monotone, the roses hang their heads. "He wants" . . . plunk-plunk . . ."bazooms" . . . plunk-plunk . . ."so pumped". . . plunk-plunk . . ."and plump". . . plunk-plunk.

I pause, my fingers trembling in C-position. I realize: If I want to keep him, my breasts go under the knife.

> after his insult
> cut rosebuds
> tightening into themselves

My threatened nipples quiver. When I'd said, "Tom, would you love me more if they were bigger?" he whined, "Baby, I wouldn't bring it up if you weren't a keeper." Now I wince at that choice of words.

> the "keeper"—
> 5-pound bass
> on the chopping board

I practice the same 12-bar blues sequence over and over.

My man, he wants some melons,
Don't wanna pick my sugar plums.
You know, my man—he wants his melons,
Ain't gonna pluck my li'l plums . . .
Gonna find me another man, honey,
Not one of these melon-suckin' bums.

It's not what I'm supposed to be practicing for my lesson, but I've got an excuse . . .

My teacher, Ivory Boy, arrives.

"Your rhythm's off," he says after he makes me do the scales again. He leans forward, flicks on the metronome. "I hate that thing," I say, not masking my irritation. I get a whiff of cheap cologne.

"It's the short guy again, isn't it?" he asks. Ivory Boy's six-foot-two.

"He wants me to have my breasts enlarged," I blurt, enjoying the shock value.

"Oh . . . I guess he's not a leg man," says Ivory Boy, a tease in his eye. Ivory Boy is 15 years younger than me. He can rip up the keys in an improvisation, but doesn't know jack about the blues. He leans back in his chair, fiddles with the metronome dial.

I can't stop myself: "A young guy like you and you're already slicing women up into body parts!" Ivory Boy's brown eyes go blank, and I realize how I sound.

"It seems important to him," I say, trying to calm down. "He made a joke once, about wanting just a handful."

Ivory Boy spreads out one hand on the keyboard, swallowing up 10 keys as he cuts a jazz lick. "Man, if I found a woman that could fill my hands, she'd need a breast reduction," he says laughing. "He sounds like a boob to me," he adds. And then, his tone turning serious, "Isn't it good you found out now that he doesn't really appreciate you?"

He slows the metronome to its largo setting. "My mother considered that operation—because she had to—and my dad and I said, "Don't bother . . ." His voice trails off. I knew his mother had died; now I know why. His eyes are like whole notes holding steady over sad chords.

I finger the keys, picking up the metronome beat. Our eyes meet again, and I feel the way I did when I first peered inside a piano, awed at the complexity of all those hammers, springs, pins and strings. I catch his eyes scanning from my neck to my waist, as if pulling down a bed sheet.

"Round your fingers," he whispers, "like you're holding a ball." He pulls at my knuckles, his touch surging through me. His voice has that low guttural tone a woman knows.

surprise
seduction
in
my
fingers
curve—
ball

I know before I make the move that this will be the end. There will be an awkward few moments afterwards and tomorrow I'll find a new piano teacher.

"You understand . . ." I say, dropping my voice with my eyes until just the right second, and then targeting his widened pupils, ". . . bite-sized is best."

Ivory Boy takes the cue, skips my mouth, and kisses me lightly on the neck. I think, I'm going to have to show this guy a thing or two, but then his left hand juts under my right shoulder blade, arching me, lengthening my throat for his wet pressing lips, scaling down my neck. He backs me against the piano. The flower vase and I crash onto the keyboard. Rose water trickles down, seeps into my jeans. Random tones amplify each shift of our bodies. His right hand is up my blouse, the tips of his big fingers teasing just one tiny point with a syncopated beat.

> long stem
> pricking me—
> I want all its scent

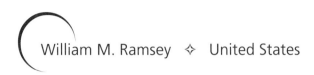

William M. Ramsey ✧ United States

Inheritance

My father is ironing wood.

In his basement workshop it is Spring 1972, and here we cannot hear the screams of Tet and Khe San, or taunts hurled at protestors marching in Boston. In silent labor, our peace and love assume form, slowly, in the veneer table he crafts step by meticulous step. Firmly I press a short length of 2x4 onto the large, heated walnut sheet, beneath which strips of waxy glue melt over white pine of the recessed table top. On the floor, in sawdust, lie large wooden vises that will clamp veneer to table while the glue sets.

I do not foresee that in twenty years I will inherit it. Indeed one day I will set books and magazines on it, seeing the wave of his hair in its sinuous grain, and write poems of pain and wonder on it. On my father's glistening hair, my poems will scrawl out their own grain and finish.

He works deliberately. Damping, sanding, staining, oiling, buffing. Loving the wood, at times caressing it so that it will sing out polished lines once sealed darkly in its weathered, annual stresses. We labor late, very late, into earth's great, chaotic night. He wants to get it right. The way it is in the grain of the pith, in its rains and droughts.

> in walnut grain
> dim sounds of war in spring–
> sap rising

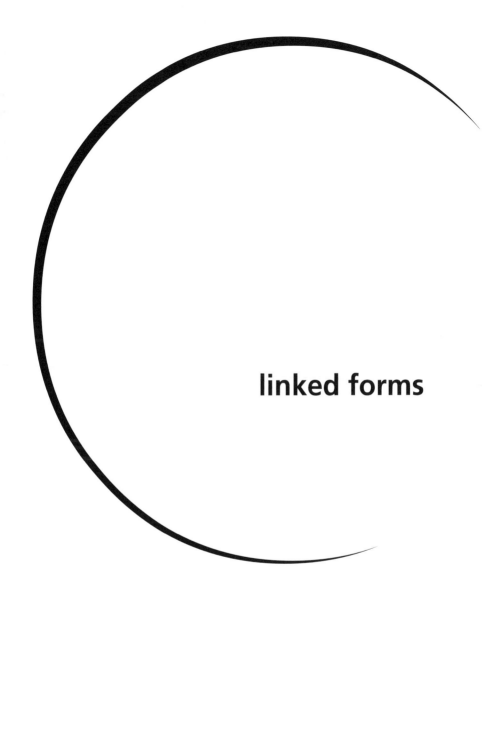

linked forms

Joann Klontz ✧ United States
Max Verhart ✧ Netherlands

Knotholes

blows of an axe
the rising groan
of a tree that falls

> a gentle rain darkens
> the cedar mulchbed

on the shelf
mahogany black
ancestors

> mother's cuckoo
> still keeping
> perfect time

magpies assembling a nest
from odd twigs and branches

> sundown
> a carpenter sips beer
> on the porch he framed

Jennifer Jensen ✧ United States
Carolyne Rohrig ✧ United States

Waxing Moon

waxing moon
the pain in my uterus
grows stronger

　　doctor visit
　　his hands all over me

a cool draught
I wipe the ultrasound gel
from my belly

　　biopsy
　　catching pieces of songs
　　from the radio

day 16
another cyst forming

　　hysterectomy
　　poring over my children's
　　baby books

Ebba Story ✧ United States
Marianna Monaco ✧ United States

Looking Twice

grove of leafless trees
  something gray flapping
    in the winter rain

again a strange sound
from the empty street

acres of tract houses
taking a wrong turn
where we once lived

whose nose
  whose face
    newborn babe

in a family bible
the list of faded names

waking at midnight
a wash of syllables
in an unknown tongue

Joann Klontz ✧ United States
Cindy Zackowitz ✧ United States

Standby

after hours
a couple side by side
in the shoeshine chairs

    someone parked
    in the yellow zone

the rattle
of the gift shop door
being shuttered

    peeking over
    the in-flight magazine
    she checks for a ring

the welcome kiosk
  unattended

    weak sunlight
    through the long windows
    baggage claim

Carolyne Rohrig ✧ United States
Marco Fraticelli ✧ Canada

Only Words

poem idea
on a napkin
in lipstick

    my note of condolence
    a run-on sentence

red
her phone card
on my dresser

    carving
    my initials
    only

under his sleeve
concentration camp number

    writer's block
    the moth
    circles my lamp

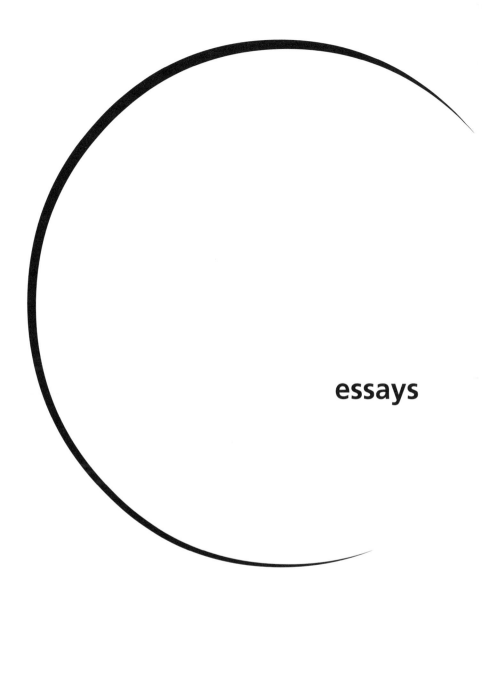

essays

Dee Evetts ✧ United States

The Conscious Eye: Homelessness

HOMELESSNESS is a topic that I have sidestepped in these pages for almost two years. This was due in part to some lingering doubts about the subject as a source or inspiration for haiku. Not on my own account, so much as given pause by opinions often strongly expressed.

At its most simplistic, the ethical or moral objection is to "making art out of other people's misfortune", thus perceived as a form of exploitation. My considered view is that the thinking behind such statements is both naive and confused. I would argue as follows. It is axiomatic that no subject under the sun is inappropriate to haiku, in particular, and to literature in general—neither vagrancy nor prostitution, not impotence, senility, or physical disablement. All are part of life's pageant, or in less purple language, what we completely and collectively are.

What matters is not the subject, but the writer's attitude. Is the reader invited to ridicule, to condescend, bolster a sense of safety and normality? Or, on the contrary, is there a spirit of enquiry, of empathy, and true compassion—founded on the underlying knowledge: there but for the grace of God go I? (Or more simply yet: *there go I*.)

I must be brief, or there will be no room left for examples. Yet in passing I want to mention a far more incisive critique, offered by John Stevenson. In a recent conversation he speculated, "Could homelessness become the cherry blossom of our time?" Now there's a disquieting question—which I shall leave hanging.

For reasons of space, I am ignoring work based on firsthand experience (Santoka, Tom Tico . . .) in order to focus on homelessness observed. Our first observer is Pamela Miller Ness:

> daybreak
> shifting his sack of cans
> shoulder to shoulder[1]

This poem stands out from the many I have received, for several reasons. There is no message or idea being paraded here. What we get is pure observation, acute and specific enough to make us feel the subject's aches and pains, and thereby to enter—however briefly—into his life predicament. The piece is all the more effective for its avoidance of the term "homeless", which being generic often hinders my perception of an individual as real as myself. (It is this formulaic aspect that troubles John Stevenson, I would guess.)

The four poems below exhibit a more standard approach to the subject. These are by Barry George, Michael Ketchek, John Dunphy, and Donald McLeod, respectively:

> After the storm
> he is rich in umbrellas
> the homeless man[2]

> windy day
> stars and stripes waving from
> homeless man's cart[3]

flophouse
beneath the ex-boxer's pillow
his scrapbook[4]

heart of the city—
a row of winos watching
the building excavation[5]

In each case the poet has taken a position that might fairly easily be paraphrased (readers may wish to try this). This is not to say that such a paraphrasing could replace the poems, for each has a life and valid-ity of its own. These pieces succeed admirably on their own terms.

Tom Painting here offers us something to be pondered longer, perhaps:

photo exhibit
faces of the homeless
in black and white[6]

This eludes any attempt at summary. By pointing to a cliché of photojournalism, the poet may be suggesting how difficult it is for most of us not to view homelessness through a lens consisting of our own prejudices and idealizations.

An unusual angle is to be found in Ed Baker's

mowing the grass
worrying
the homeless[7]

Here there is interaction as well as observation. A feeling of tension arises from the potential conflict of interests—a collision of worlds usually held apart. The poem is not devoid of humor, which also works in its favor.

The same can be said of this comically forlorn picture evoked by David Cobb:

> cathedral front—
> a drop-out sits with angels
> made of stone[8]

He has conjured up uncannily my own memories of sleeping rough in Europe, after abandoning university. This was not real homelessness, to be sure. Yet a sufficient taste of it to glimpse how even vagrancy contains a lure that could become compelling. And this is the aspect that most unsettles us, I suspect, undermining as it does the sense of substance and identity conferred by our houses and apartments.

A suitable *envoie* is provided by Charlotte Digregorio, with this very quiet poem:

> fog blankets
> the downtown bridge. . .
> homeless man vanishes[9]

As easily and anonymously as this the homeless slip from sight, and from our thoughts.

------

1. unpublished
2. *Point Judith Light*, Spring-Summer 1999
3. *Raw NerVZ Haiku*, Vol. V, No 2
4. unpublished
5. unpublished
6. unpublished
7. unpublished

Kai Falkman ✧ Sweden

Construction & Distortion of the Image in Haiku

In the beginning of the 1960s I read R. H. Blyth's translations of Japanese haiku. It was a rewarding introduction to the Japanese language and to Japanese literature. I did not notice at the time that the reason for the flatness of many poems very often was that Blyth had transposed the order of the three lines.

In the 1980s I realized that not only Blyth but other translators as well often changed the story of the haiku by transposing lines. An example:

> *Kamo arite*
> *mizu made ayumu*
> *kori kana*

This haiku by Ransetsu is translated by Blyth thus:

> The wild ducks there
> walk across the ice
> up to the water

Blyth comments that this poem is "too explanatory and matter-of-fact." But the original has a point which the translation misses:

> Wild ducks
> walk up to the water
> over the ice

When we read the first two lines we imagine the wild ducks walking up to the water on land. In the third line we suddenly have to switch our view and replace the land with ice. It is this rapid change of image which gives the poem its surprising point.
Another example:

> *To-yama ga*
> *medama ni utsuru*
> *tonbo kana*

This haiku by Issa is translated by Harold G. Henderson in his well-known book *An Introduction to Haiku:*

> In its eye
> are mirrored far-off mountains—
> dragonfly!

The first line in Henderson's translation tells us nothing. Our gaze is given no concrete image on which to fix. Whose eye?

Already in the second line the point is revealed, as the reader sees the mountains reflected in an eye.

The image of the dragonfly in the third line explains whose eye it is, thus completing the picture. But its dramatic effect has been diluted by the separation of the eye and the dragonfly.

In the Japanese original the first line shows the mountains in the distance. In the second line this image shifts and the mountains appear reflected in an eye, which we finally discover to be the eye of a dragonfly.

Blyth reproduces the correct sequence:

> The distant mountains
> are reflected in the pupils
> of the dragonfly.

These examples demonstrate the importance in haiku of the image structure. If parts of the picture are transposed, its meaning alters and the point is lost.

Each word in haiku is a building block in the construction of an image—if the place of the word is changed in the translation, the construction collapses. The construction of the image determines the vision of the reader and the feelings evoked by the vision. Haiku has the structure of a drama—you cannot change the order of the acts. The first line sets the scene, often with an image of tranquility such as a pond, a mountain, an autumn moon, or perhaps a close-up of a flower, a dragonfly, a parasol.

The second line describes the action or movement. The picture comes alive.

The third line reveals the meaning of the action or movement: it lets us see what it is that has caused the change. This is the element of the surprise, of insight.

Here is an elegant example that illustrates the mechanism of surprise in haiku:

> *Yuki tokete*
> *mura ippai no*
> *kodomo kana*
> *Issa*

> Snow melts,
> and the village is overflowing—
> with children
> *(Henderson)*

The second line excites the imagination: there is so much melting snow that the village is flooded. The third line brings the surprise: with children. When the threatening image of the torrential waters gives way to the happy image of children, our presentiment of disaster is replaced by a feeling of relief and joy. The transformation of the image transforms the feeling.

In haiku the point often consists of a shift in perspective. The distant mountains are reflected in the eye of the dragonfly. The image is reduced or enlarged, or placed within an unexpected frame, as in Issa's

> Dai-butsu no
> hana kara izuru
> tsubame kana

> Out from the hollow
> of the Great Buddha's nose—
> comes a swallow
> (Henderson)

This haiku was written when the poet was looking at the great statue of Buddha at Nara. In the English translation, however, we never see the Buddha in its entirety. To start with we see a *hollow*, and the Buddha's *nose*, from which a *swallow* flies out.

The original sequence of the image runs:

> The Great Buddha's
> nose from comes out
> a swallow

Freely translated:

> The Great Buddha—
> from its nose
> darts a swallow

Another example:

> Yamadera no
> homotsu miru ya
> hana no ame
> *Kyoshi*

> Rain on the cherry blossoms;
> looking at the treasures
> in the mountain temple
> *(Blyth)*

The reader's gaze fastens first on the cherry blossoms and then on the treasures of the temple—can this have been the poet's intention? The original sequence of images is:

> In the mountain temple
> we look at the treasures—
> raining cherry blossoms

The poet's gaze rises from the treasures to the petals falling like raindrops outside the mountain temple. *Hana no ame* can be translated as *rain on* or *raining cherry blossoms*—the important point is that the image of nature's treasures comes last.

> Yukiore ya
> mukashi ni kaeru
> kasa no hone
> *Shoi*

> Broken with snow,
> the frame of the bamboo umbrella
> reveals its original form
> *(Blyth)*

The picture undergoes a very suggestive transform-
ation in this haiku. The snow has broken a bamboo
umbrella, but the snow also allows the original form
of the umbrella to emerge. The umbrella is taken
apart and put together again before our inner eye,
although in reality the broken frame lies abandoned
in the snow. The whole transformation takes place
in the reader's mind.

The sequence of images in the original is another,
but in this case I wonder whether Blyth's version is
not preferable. The original—it seems to me—
requires a mental lap backwards, to the second line,
before the point can be fully grasped.

> Broken with snow
> the form reappears
> of the umbrella frame

A haiku by Rinka:

> *Rokugatsu-kaze*
> *haka no ushiro mo*
> *kage wa nashi*

Translation by Blyth:

> The June breeze:
> No shadow of anyone
> behind the grave

The sequence of images in the original runs:

> The June breeze
> Behind the grave
> no shadow

Haiku presents us with three images—here, a fourth image is evoked in the reader's mind. The gravestone leaves no shadow (image 3), the sun is high in the sky (image 4). The fourth image does not emerge clearly in Blyth's interpretation, which ends with the darkness of the grave.

Furthermore, Blyth has personified the shadow: *No shadow of anyone.* This interpretation has no justification in the original. Implicitly the image of *shadow* contains a suggestion of the human in this context, but the impact is weakened by the explicit statement.

The final impression of the original is one of light: the June wind has blown the clouds from the sun and driven away the shadow of the dead.

This is a very important point, often overlooked by translators: Contrasts between darkness and light in haiku generally end with the light. A genuine haiku almost always closes with a sense of optimism and universality.

We have been exploring the affect transposition of images has on haiku, and how translators of haiku into English have mistaken some classical poems by such transposition. An example by Kyoroku:

> *Hito-sao wa*
> *shinishozoku ya*
> *doyo-boshi*

Translation by Blyth:

> Summer airing:
> On one of the poles,
> death-clothes

Here, the prelude is light in tone, the finale dark. The sequence of images in the original creates a different mood:

> On a post
> mourning clothes—
> summer airing

A poem by Gyodai:

> *Hana kurete*
> *tsuki wo idakeri*
> *haku-botan*

Translation by Blyth:

> The flowers darken
> but the white peony
> absorbs the moonlight

The sequence of images in the original runs:

> The flowers darken,
> the moon is absorbed
> by the white peony

The surprise is the white peony, not the moonlight. The whiteness of the peony is emphasized by the moon, and the peony appears as a bright light in the darkness. The moon and the peony are two round poles united by a beam of light.

In Blyth's version the peony is not truly white in the second line; the *but* detracts from the brightness of the flower. In the third line the moonlight appears, but by that time the memory of the peony is already growing fainter. And our thoughts rebel against returning to the second line, to let the moonlight include the peony in its flow.

Each line in a true haiku opens the door to the next line—the third line opens the door to a surprising revelation, to an insight. The mind does not want to go back.

Iza kaite
atsusa wasuren
Fuji no yuki
        Kisoku

Well, I'll draw
the snow of Mount Fuji,
to forget the heat!
        (Blyth)

Our thoughts make a great leap from the drawing block to the top of the mountain, only to return abruptly to the heat of the plain. This causes confusion and disappointment.

The sequence of images in the original is:

I shall draw
to forget the heat
the snow of Fuji

The second line is interesting because it gives a dynamic overtone to the opening words: we understand the effort of will with which the poet has decided to do something—to draw—to escape the excruciating heat which is making him listless and tired. In the third line comes the leap to the top of Mount Fuji, where the white snow has a strong cooling effect.

A well-known haiku by Buson:

Ja wo kitte
wataru tanima no
wakaba kana

Translation by Blyth:

> Young leaves of the valley
> I passed through
> after killing a snake!

The original produces quite a different mood:

> The snake is killed
> I travel through the ravine's
> young leaves

The dramatic event opens the poem, but the reader is also told that the action belongs to the past, which softens the violence of the emotion. In the second line we are led away from the snake but still in the ravine which retains an uncanny atmosphere. The third line is light and hopeful: *young leaves.*

Sight and sound play important contrasting roles in haiku, e.g. in Basho's *The old pond*, where the jump of the frog evokes a visual image in the reader's mind but is described with an audible image by the poet: *the sound of water.* Another well-known poem by Basho is this one:

> *Shizukasa ya*
> *iwa ni shimiiru*
> *semi no koe*

> Silence
> Cutting into the cliff
> the cry of the cicada

This poem has been included in Donald Keene's *Japanese Literature, An Introduction to Western Readers,* and has been translated as follows:

> Such stillness—
> the cries of the cicadas
> sink into the rock

The silence emerges more clearly without the addition of *such*. Already in the second line the silence is broken bye *the cries of the cicadas*. The transition is too sharp to nourish he imagination or the emotions—such sharp transitions generally occur between the second and third lines. In the third line the audible image becomes visual—the cries *sink into the rock*—but the point is undermined because the link between the rock and the silence has been broken.

Henderson retains the sequence of the original:

> So still:
> Into rocks it pierces—
> the locust-shrill

Stillness would have been more effective than *so still*. The word *it* in the second line points forward and seems unnecessary, but perhaps the order of the words in English requires it. Henderson uses the singular, which seems logical. It is unlikely that several cicadas would break the silence together. However, contrary to Keene, Henderson uses the plural for *iwa* (rock, cliff), which perhaps is too imprecise for this haiku.

These observations do not intend to deride the translations by Blyth, Henderson and others, which generally are most faithful to the original texts. Sometimes changes in the positions of the words are necessary in order to render the original into intelligible English. However, to change the order of the lines is very risky, because it changes the construction of the image and thereby misses the meaning of the poem and the feeling that the poet wants to evoke. It is surprising that an experienced translator of haiku like R. H. Blyth often did not seem to realize this.

In a few cases Blyth's liberty in transposing the lines can make his version better than the original:

Natsu-kusa ni
kikansha no sharin
kite tomaru
    Seishi

The wheel of the locomotive
comes and stops
by the summer grass
    (Blyth)

Literally translated, the original would run:

By the summer grass
the wheel of the locomotive
comes and stops

The picture is complete and the meaning revealed already in the second line. All the third line does is to add a little to the imagination.

Recent translations of haiku seem to be more careful in transposing the lines. The translators of the first book of English translations devoted to a woman haiku master, *Chiyo-ni* (Tuttle Publishing, 1998), Patricia Donegan and Yoshie Ishibashi, state in the preface that they have tried to retain the original line order and order of images. When they, in a few cases, choose to abandon this rule, the meaning of the original image is damaged. An example:

Yugao ya
mono no kakurete
utsukushiki

Moonflowers—
the beauty
of hidden things

The second and the third lines have changed places. *Moonflowers* should, of course, be followed by the reference to *hidden things,* as the moonflower blooms in dusk, unfolding its whiteness faintly at first and more so as the night darkens.

Another haiku by Chiyo-ni:

> *Hana no ka ni*
> *ushiro misete ya*
> *koromogae*

Translated as:

> Change of kimono:
> showing only her back
> to the blossom's fragrance

Here, the translators have placed the point of the poem, the revealing explanation—*change of kimono*—in the first line instead of in the third line, while *the blossom's fragrance* should open the poem. The fragrance of the blossom is a subtle reference to the seasonal change of kimono from the winter to summer. The fragrance is present throughout the poem even if Chiyo-ni discretely turns her back to the unnamed flower.

As is evident from these several examples, the preservation of the original order in haiku is critical to retaining the poet's intention. Such liberties should be taken at the translator's risk, and rarely to his credit. From these examples, too, we can gather the value of being aware of the order of images in our own original poems, how they open and unfold, one following the other, to create the moment of surprise that we associate with the very best moments of haiku.

Richard Gilbert ✧ Japan

Universalism v. Particularism in International Haiku

ON THE CUTTING EDGE of the world-stage, international haiku is possibly the first actively global poetic form, to judge by the number of books, sites, conferences, and associations that are currently being promulgated. There are some interesting parallels between the international haiku movement and other globalizing forces: GATT, NAFTA, and the WTO (inciting international protests, emblematic of large-scale concern), the internet, and global media networks. Generally speaking, we are witnessing an increasing polarization of local v. non-local paradigms.

We need to consider carefully the effects of a globalization of haiku. The power of these effects can't be underestimated. On the one hand, how powerful is it, that through the publication of a book like *Knots: The Anthology of Southeastern European Haiku Poetry* (US Distributor: Red Moon Press, 1999), poems such as:

> spring evening—
> the wheel of a troop carrier
> crushes a lizard
> *Anakiev Dimitar, Slovenia*

> moonlit lake
> the muzzle of a deer
> touches water
> *Banea Stefan, Romania*

a single stone
protrudes from the grass—
our former home
Dadic Rade, Yugoslavia

give a human face, a sensitive, compassionate heart
to the peoples of this region, at a time when billions
are bombarded with wanton media images of killing
and destruction. The poetry of *Knots* gives us, as well
as many great haiku, a way of finding each other
across differences, politics, national and cultural
boundaries. And, these poems and essays become all
the stronger tied together under the aegis of a
singular, landmark publication.

One can immediately grasp the space of heart we
all share.

In terms of particulars, the most obvious
particular is language. We need to further consider
methods of presentation that allow us some contact
with the poetic play of "local" languages (including
international varieties of English), which we are not
privy to. We face complex translation issues in works
that take an international approach to haiku—thus
the reader of *Knots* can appreciate the elegant fluidity
of the English translations—an instance of particulars
universalizing so that these particulars can become
available and grasped throughout the world. *Knots*
is an example of achievement in international haiku
that brings us a means, as multiple peoples sharing
a planet together, of breaking through stereotypes
and emotional remove, or simply ignorance,
regarding communities, peoples and conditions
typically witnessed partially, at a great distance.

There is a darker side of universalism as well,
which I am relating with internationalism, or
globalism. Now that haiku as an international
phenomenon has left its nest of Japan and is
permeating through the global sieve, what we stand

to lose is the local. There is tension between the need to communicate to the widest possible global audience or reader, and the local particulars of language, culture, custom, season, flora, fauna, etc. We need to further examine the question of locality and particulars as we globalize, in terms of the presentation, and also the overall arena of international haiku. Especially, there are issues of commonality, in terms of communication seeking a lowest common denominator of accessible comprehensibility, with its implied detriments. To cite one of many themes, how many "foreign" (the term itself an evolving paradox) place names and other references can or should we allow into international haiku presentations? Let's consider an example. Perhaps you are familiar with Marpa, a major icon of Tibetan Buddhist culture. How should we present a haiku such as,

> the moon fainter
> over Marpa point—
> dry grass whispers

Several editors have suggested that the author change "Marpa" to a more universally familiar term of location, such as "North." This might be acceptable editorial advice within the purview of a purely Anglo/national haiku format. In fact, it has generally been an unofficial guideline to disallow terminology that is relatively unfamiliar or non-comprehensible to one's main audience. I would maintain however, that changing "Marpa" to "North" universalizes the haiku at the expense of its particularized core: an act of local culture and context. Given that the above haiku is acceptable without alteration, should the haiku be annotated? If so, how might this best be accomplished? These are areas that may require conceptual expansion and reconsideration.

Further, one can beg the question of what haiku is. The non-local really means non-body, non-season, and non-space. This is one face of the Internet (e.g. Swatch Internet World-time). The waxing force of the non-local perspective is also represented by world trade agreements. One reason for current international protest is that, in effect, the earlier-mentioned trade agreements encourage an internationalized economy which seeks the lowest common denominator of price while ignoring local concerns, arguably abetting the destruction of patterns of cultural and biotic life integral to local communities. In fact, it may be that an international poetic form such as haiku, historically rooted in the genius of Japanese culture, is one of the few places where particulars of place, person, culture, and custom can be heard and felt directly.

At its outset, the six volume *Cambridge History of Japan* defines one of three foundational paradigms of Japanese culture as particularism, introducing their exegesis on a cautionary note: "Particularism stands poles apart from the universalism of such world religions as Buddhism and Christianity . . . at the core of this paradigm lies the old and lasting belief that every *kami* (even though invisible) resides in one sacred object located at one particular place (vol. 1:16)." R. H. Blyth, in *A History of Haiku,* vehemently argues against an aesthetic that seeks to distill universal truths from haiku particulars: "[Basho] is saying that each thing is, not has, infinite value. There is no separation between the thing and its meaning, no finding the universal in particular natural objects or human beings (vol. 1:14)."

It may be argued that poetic particulars have little to do with world trade, and that it is an over-generalization from the sort of universalism indicated in the paragraph above, to the problematics of internationalism.

However, similar linkages have been articulated in the works of Octavio Paz and Morris Berman (just for starters), which for reasons of brevity cannot be detailed here. Poetry in general utilizes a language of particulars, and especially in haiku we may want to pay attention to the question of preserving these manifold particulars, as haiku are "internationalized" through translation into English, uprooted from their homelands (through the net and international publication), and modified, even commodified, to fit the contingencies of universal access.

These are issues that have existed in discussions of the English-language haiku for some time, but are now taking on an even greater importance. Because haiku come from the earth, from a particularized poetic ground wedded to an ecos of locality, it seems timely to consider issues relating to preservation, the 'what' and 'how,' in terms of haiku selection and presentation on the international stage.

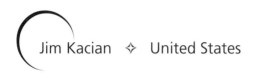

Jim Kacian ✧ United States

Beyond Kigo:
Haiku in the Next Millennium

IN AUGUST 1999 the First International Haiku Symposium was held in Tokyo. Over two hundred Japanese haijin, as well as representatives of English-French- and German-speaking haiku poets attended. The event was occasioned by what is per-ceived to be, in Japan at any rate, a crisis in haiku, as well as the realization that haiku is now the most practiced form of literature in the world. The hope was that some consensus of what the haiku of the future may look like might be achieved. A further consideration for the Japanese was, what role would it be advantageous for them to take on in the burgeoning of the form far beyond the constraints of its cultural hegemony. These are not light questions: haiku is arguably Japan's foremost cultural export, and to watch it proliferate in foreign cultures without influencing its propagation is tantamount to letting it find its own course. This means having no influence on how it might grow in the future outside of the work of its individual poets as exemplars of excellence in the form—in short, an equal influence to the rest of the world.

Several issues were discussed, most notably what is essential to haiku as it is currently understood. While the usual and expected range of opinions on syllable counting and appropriate content was present, it is interesting to note that the element most vehemently attacked, and defended, was the issue of *kigo*. This is most fitting, I believe, since *kigo* are bound up with the very nature of what a haiku is in a way that no amount of counting ever could be: *kigo* carry the cargo of the cultural perception of Japan. It may be true that the rhythm of the speech of the Japanese is reflected in its poetic forms as well as advertising, sloganeering and much else, but *kigo* are an evocation of the way the Japanese people perceive their universe. It is no wonder they might be loathe to forego this understanding as the underpinning of the form they created. If they surrender this, what about the form remains essentially Japanese?

Conferences rarely solve such matters, and it was no different here. Nevertheless, the fact that such issues are being discussed at all suggests an awareness that was not present in the international haiku community only a few years ago. What was assumed to be inviolate up until very recently has now come under questioning. This reflects, I believe, the fact that so many people are writing haiku today, in so many different places, with so many different needs and such different content to convey. And since haiku has become so international, it is fitting that these matters come under consideration, so that what is truly essential and universal in the form may be distinguished from what is merely local.

The preceding articles of this volume have explored the element of *kigo*, how they function, how essential they are. What I wish to discuss here are some alternatives to *kigo*, and what the implications of choosing such alternatives might be to the future of haiku.

There is no question that *kigo* have been indispensable in the development of the classical Japanese haiku. Further, they have supplied the most important structural element in a form where structure is most exposed. *Kigo* make it possible for poems to open outward, to call upon the broadest possible range of human experience within the context where this experience is encountered. Haiku as it has developed is inconceivable without the existence of a formal system of *kigo* to brace it up.

However, it is incontestable that the Japanese experience and expression of climatic, geological, astronomical, not to say personal, conditions cannot be universal, any more than the European or American experience may be. Since haiku aspires to international status, the element which permits them to open must not be limited to the truths and observations of a single culture, but must be amenable to a more universal inclusiveness. Further, it must remain open-ended, to permit growth from subsequent input from other cultures and experiences not yet attending haiku.

That said, I believe *kigo* will continue to matter in haiku in all cultures. They are the leavening which makes the dough of haiku rise. Nearly all people have had the experience of rain, of wind, of snow or drought, and nearly all have at least heard or seen pictures of tornado and flood. It is this shared experience which makes such elements work for so many people. What may not be so apparent is the value placed upon such elements in different cultures. The onset of rain means something completely different to people in India, in England, in the Pacific Northwest. Yet it would be reasonable to expect the poets of these regions to write their haiku based on such experiences in English. It seems unlikely that the same *kigo* would suffice for each of them.

Further, the diversity of climate within a large country, the United States for example, means that any meteorological or climatic event meant to speak for an entire culture would perforce occur at different times within the same culture—even if we grant the culture is uniform within its geographical boundaries,

127

which is patently not the case.

What we want, then, is a *kigo* which is not restricted in its meaning. Cherry blossoms, to use a well-worn example, will connote spring in the specific clime where the poet resides, even if it does not suggest March 15, say, in all cases. If we lose a bit of precision, we gain an inclusiveness. And most importantly, in this model poets take their cue from nature, rather than the other way around. A *saijiki* does not decide when cherry blossoms will appear, but merely records the previous experiences of close observers. Our own close observation may be added to the rest, often reinforcing what others have found, sometimes surprising us with an aberrant timing. In any case, the *saijiki* should be consulted to place the observations of the poet within a context, not to determine when an event, and a poem, ought to take place. And a *saijiki* is nothing more than a collection of *kigo*.

Kigo will continue to proliferate. There is not a fixed limit to the number of perceptions of life we might have. When there is a new perception or means of expression, it is not burdensome to add a new *kigo* to the list. At the same time, it is not important that *kigo* be presented in any fashion which intends to be exhaustive, as in, for example, a *saijiki*. The only people who might be concerned about the proliferation of *kigo* are *saijiki* editors and publishers.

The natural cycles and their poetic counterparts, *kigo*, will continue to be used in haiku for the foreseeable future, since they continue to offer so much structure and breadth to poems. But is it possible for other structural elements to be as useful to the poet as these have been? Or for the old elements to be used in new ways?

Any replacement for *kigo* must function in the same fashion as *kigo*, that is, must be omnipresent and yet particular, emotive and yet self-contained, suggestive and yet free, expansive and yet confinable; in short, a replacement for *kigo* must contain as much information and structure as *kigo* do. Or else, such a replacement must function in some completely different fashion. I do not mean to be simplistic here: what I am suggesting is that *kigo* are perfectly suited to the function they perform, and a replacement must replace it exactly or enlarge upon it, or else the whole notion must be reconsidered and an entirely different set of parameters chosen instead of those which have determined haiku to this point. It is debatable, of course, whether the products of such a choice will also be called haiku.

So let us, then, explore two paths: exact or enlarged replacement; and complete alternative.

The fact is, there would be no need to replace *kigo* with anything if it was truly inclusive. But it is not: there are hundreds of poems which look and function like haiku, indeed are haiku, which do not contain *kigo*. Sometimes these are shrugged off as "serious senryu" or "non seasonal haiku," but this begs the question. How can a poem be a haiku if it doesn't include all the elements of haiku? Either we must conclude that it's not a haiku, or else our notion of what must be included in a haiku must be adjusted.

In truth, *kigo* are not exhaustive. They are not the only context in which we might experience what we call a "haiku moment." And so haiku are written without *kigo*—but what do they contain?

What such poems contain may be called *keywords*. The keyword is a near kin to a season word. In fact, it may be a season word. But it may be other things as well.

The most useful way of thinking of the idea of keywords is not as a one-to-one replacement for *kigo*, but rather as an overarching system of correspondences available to the haiku poet which incorporates *kigo* within its bounds. Consider, for example

moonlight
river divides the forest
into two nights
Nikola Nilic

What we would have done in the past is to call this a
non seasonal haiku, or else assign it a season. It
certainly could have been written in any season, and
to place it in the "Winter" season, for example,
would be arbitrary at best. This is the way we have
worked within the mindset of *kigo* .

In the new way of reckoning, however, a *kigo* is
not an assumed part of a haiku, but a keyword is. A
word or phrase which opens up of the poem is
employed, in this case "moonlight". There are thou-
sands of others, including all the known *kigo*. The
poem, then, is a haiku employing a keyword, with a
seasonal feeling (since it is a natural event being
described) but not a definite seasonal attribution, or
kigo. *Kigo*, then, operate as one large and important
subset of all keywords, but are not the only words
which a haiku may employ to the same effect.

Consider some poems from the recent
international compendium *Knots: The Anthology of
Southeast European Haiku Poetry*. While there is cer-
tainly plenty of "spring rain" and "autumn sky" as
there ought to be, there are also poems such as these:

my best friend died—   deserted town—
some tiny grains of dust   hungry war victims
on our chessboard   feed the pigeons
        Robert Bebek   Mile Stamenkovic

These poems choose obvious and important subjects
for their haiku moments. They are closely observed,
have a moment of insight, have an emotive core
which touches the reader. Few people would argue
that they are not some sort of haiku, even though

they do not contain *kigo*. But clearly "dust" and "victims" work in an analogous way here, and are the pivot and purpose of the poetry. These are not non seasonal anything. They are poems that work in the tradition of haiku which call upon a larger context than even *kigo* can supply for their impact. Recognizing and exploiting this is one of the chief characteristics of much of contemporary international, including Japanese, work. It seems somewhat beside the point to insist upon the one, when the other, more inclusive, covers the situation. There are many, many more such examples as these in *Knots* and in other contemporary books and journals of haiku.

Keywords, then, can replace the notion of *kigo* completely, and successfully, without radically altering the nature of haiku as we know it. And this is a successful, perhaps the only possible successful, means of doing so.

However, another alternative is also being tried, though perhaps less successfully to this point. *Kigo* attempt to embody an entire ethos within their structure, and so it would make sense that a replacement for *kigo* must substitute its own ethos for that of the natural cycle. And in fact there are many examples of such attempts: the internet is littered with them. They range from the ludicrous, as in spam-ku, to niche interests with vampire-ku and gothic-ku, to entire alternative worlds in sci-fi-ku, and many other subgenres as well.

These alternatives are not regarded very highly by the "serious" haiku community, and to the present I would say with good reason. Not much of the work which has been produced by these alternatives seems to be worthy of much attention. But I think it would be a mistake to disdain them altogether. It is not difficult to imagine that a truly powerful literary mind might indeed take up one of these spheres and

131

make it his or her own, and in so doing utilize the resources available in such alternative universes, particularly in sci-fi-ku. If this seems a ridiculous argument, I suggest that it is no more farfetched than other artistic endeavors which have no necessary analog with the "real" world but contain their own internal logic and necessity, such as music or chess. While these disciplines may not appeal to all, those who do engage in them find them compellingly real, worthy of much study and endeavor, and consider the finest results beautiful and true and inevitable in the same way we might consider a poem to be.

In the next millennium, then, international haiku will have dispensed with the notion of *kigo* in favor of the more overarching concept of keyword. This process is more evolutionary than revolutionary. Through such a development haiku will continue to be grounded in a universal system of value which is communicable to its practitioners and readership; there will be a smooth transition since none of the "classics" of haiku need be thrown out due to the adoption of radically new values; and new work which speaks to a far larger and perhaps more contemporary audience will find acceptance within the canon of haiku because of the enlarged understanding of how such poems function. And it is possible that one of the niche forms of haiku will have become the personal provenance of a truly unique sensibility, which might further restructure the way we look at haiku. It will be interesting to watch these developments over the coming decades as our old haiku becomes new. And this is necessary, since an unchanging art is a moribund art. Haiku, beginning its new international life, is anything but.

Ban'ya Natsuishi ✧ Japan

Common Ground: The Basis for World Haiku in the 21ˢᵗ Century

THERE ARE MANY PROBLEMS with world haiku, which at first might appear quite easy to resolve, but in truth prove quite difficult. Sometimes it is the truth in which are lives are engaged which proves elusive: for example, take the seemingly simple question, does all humanity trace itself to a common ancestral mother, the so-called "African Eve"? Perhaps it might be worth considering this question, before we discuss our common basis for world haiku.

I am no anthropologist, and of course cannot give a definitive conclusion to our question. But if we have an "African Eve" as our sole ancestral mother, then it is easy to find a basis for world haiku. If, however, there are multiple ancestral mothers— "African Eve", "Asian Eve", and so on—then it is not so easy to argue for a commonality in haiku, or anything else, for that matter. In any case, however, we know we must hold some things in common. We exchange genes, after all, with the birth of every child. These, and other elements, lie beyond any secondary differences.

One of these elements (and I could choose hundreds) which I would like to discuss here is "dreaming". Not only human beings, but other animals as well, are capable of dreaming during sleep. Dreaming may be indispensable to the health of some living creatures. Dreams also play important roles in many myths, legends and folktales from

133

around the world. For example, the ancient Egyptians (among others) considered dreams to be divine revelations. In the Christian and Jewish world, the dreams of Solomon and Jacob are universally known. In the mythology of my own Japanese heritage, Takakuraja was urged in a dream to help the future first Japanese Emperor, Jinmu, to unify ancient Japan. There are many others. I do not advocate a return to the beliefs of an ancient mindset, but I do urge you all to not the continuing importance of dreams to humanity.

I'm very interested in contemporary haiku in which the word "dream" is featured. Here's an American haiku, taken from the "All Year" chapter of Haiku World (Kodansha, 1996) edited by William J. Higginson:

> restless dream
> a game of hide and seek
> in the graveyard
> *Joanne Morcom, USA*

I like this for the expression "restless dream", which has the same sincerity as each of our lives has.

Among contemporary Japanese haiku submitted to *Our Dream* (Ginyu Press, 2000, edited by Sagicho Aihara and myself), the following centered on dreams and dreaming:

> As numerous as
> thorns of the cactus—
> my dreams
> *Sumie Aihara, Japan*

> In my dream
> float
> all shapes and sizes
> *Saki Inui, Japan*

Sumie Aihara recognizes her many bitter dreams. Saki Inui (an 11-year-old girl) is surprised at her confused dream. Indeed, both poets have succeeded in seizing upon some critical truth through their dreams.

I have published recently, in "Ginyu" #8 (a haiku journal which I edit), the following two poems focused on dreams, in both of which I find a deep attraction in my heart:

Mlada trava . . .   The young grasses . . .
Planina krvari iz slema   The mountain bleeds from
                                          a helmet
Punog snova   Full of dreams
                Dimitar Anakiev, Slovenia

Alluding to one of the most famous of Basho's haiku "Natsukusa ya", Anakiev skillfully expresses the miserableness of the war dead. In a way that is true to life, the word "dreams" shows us the future possibilities erased by war. I suppose that the poet composed it based upon his own war experiences in the former Yugoslavia. His haiku is certainly realistic, but what matters most is its universality. Even a man who doesn't know the details of this war (or any other) can understand the truths it contains: both the cruelty of war and the beauty of the landscape are given us at the same time. In this way, it avoids being propagandistic, and is, instead, poetic.

Anakiev may have been inspired equally by the former battle fields of World War I where more than one million young soldiers were killed. I would like to offer the following haiku to these young dead, to let them take a restful peace:

135

Behind a rock
on the green slope
dead soldiers' spirits
Ban'ya Natsuishi

Another touching haiku focused on dreams and alluding to war is this one, taken from *Parce Neba: Haiku iz sklonista* (*A Piece of the Sky: Haiku from an air-raid shelter*, Prijatelj Press, 1999, ed. Dimitar Anakiev):

US-bomb US-pakao	US-bomb US-hell
U decijim snovima	in children's dreams
Zasto Srbija?	why Serbia?

Miroslav Klivar, Czech Republic

Placed on the second line, the word "dreams" serves as a center of any relations among the words appearing in this haiku. More precisely, "children's dreams" is a crucial acknowledgment of all the miseries of people, young and old, unhappily involved in the war.

Contrary to these two haiku composed in southeastern Europe, the following smart example is quite refreshing.

into my dreams
the gentle rocking
of the ship
Jim Kacian, USA

Here the poet's "dream" grows gentle and relaxed by the healing movement of the waves of the sea. Through haiku composed in several lang-uages, we can reach various essential aspects of "dream". Thus the non-seasonal keyword "dream" is an excellent means of showing that common ground which humanity shares, and which serves as the basis for world haiku.

Two contradictory principles are always at work in any haiku. First: brevity, instantaneity, concentration; second: duration, continuity, undulation. The most important element of the first principle is the keyword, whether it concerns the seasons or more fundamental matters for humanity or the universe. We should not abandon all season words as worthless or lacking creative energy. But if we are to truly enter the age of world haiku, they cannot remain the absolute center of haiku.

There is no standard time or climate: we can fully enjoy the various and local conditions and still place them within the rubric of world haiku. But we also need a rich basis, a common ground, to keep world haiku from becoming prosaic and trivial.

At present, we cannot be certain of the entirety of the basis for the future of world haiku. However, there are many aspects, such as our consideration of "dream", which seem quite rich. One hundred keywords would not illustrate the whole, but might suggest the breadth and value of it. I reassert that we hold some things in common that lie beyond our secondary differences, such as nationalities, religions, languages, tastes, passions, ages, and so forth.

Though the totality of the basis for world haiku is not yet revealed, it can be found here and there. So one of the dreams we hold in common, the future of world haiku, seems quite promising, as suggested by the following haiku by one of the most brilliant of Japanese haiku masters:

> Slept well
> till the withered field in my dream
> turned green
> *Tohta Kaneko, Japan*

Prof. Haruo Shirane ✧ United States

Beyond the Haiku Moment:
Basho, Buson, and Modern Haiku Myths

WHAT DOES NORTH AMERICAN HAIKU look like when observed from Japan? What kind of advice might haiku masters such as Bashō and Buson give to English haiku poets? What would Bashō and Buson say if they were alive today and could read English and could read haiku done by North American poets?

I think that they would be delighted to find that haiku had managed to cross the Pacific and thrive so far from its place of origin. They would be impressed with the wide variety of haiku composed by North American haiku poets and find their work most innovative. At the same time, however, they would also be struck, as I have been, by the narrow definitions of haiku found in haiku handbooks, magazines, and anthologies. I was once told that Ezra Pound's famous Metro Poem, first published in 1913, was not haiku.

> The apparition of these faces in the crowd:
> Petals on a wet, black bough.

If I remember correctly, the reason for disqualification was that the Metro poem was not about nature as we know it and that the poem was fictional or imaginary. Pound's poem may also have been ruled out since it uses an obvious metaphor: the petals are a metaphor for the apparition of the faces, or vice versa. This view of the Metro poem was based on three key definitions of haiku—haiku is about direct observation, haiku eschews metaphor, and haiku is about nature—which poets such as Bashō and Buson would have seriously disputed.

Haiku as Direct Personal Experience or Observation

One of the widespread beliefs in North America is that haiku should be based on one's own direct experience, that it must derive from one's own observations, particularly of nature. But it is important to remember that this is basically a modern view of haiku, the result, in part, of nineteenth century European realism, which had an impact on modern Japanese haiku and then was re-imported back to the West as something very Japanese. Bashō, who wrote in the seventeenth century, would not have made such a distinction between direct personal experience and the imaginary, nor would he have placed higher value on fact over fiction.

Bashō was first and foremost a master of haikai, or comic linked poetry. In haikai linked verse, the seventeen syllable *hokku*, or opening verse, is followed by a 14 syllable *wakiku*, or added verse, which in turn is followed by the seventeen syllable third verse, and so forth. Except for the first verse, which stood alone, each additional verse was read together with the previous verse and pushed away from the penultimate verse, or the verse prior to the previous verse. Thus, the first and second verse, the second and third verse, third and fourth verse formed independent units, each of which pushed off from the previous unit.

The joy and pleasure of haikai was that it was imaginary literature, that the poets who participated in linked verse moved from one world to the next, across time, and across space. The basic idea of linked verse was to create a new and unexpected world out of the world of the previous verse. One could compose about one's daily life, about being an official in China, about being a warrior in the medieval period, or an aristocrat in the ancient period. The other participants in the haikai sequence joined you in that imaginary world or took you to places that you could reach only with your imagination.

One of the reasons that linked verse became so popular in the late medieval period, in the fifteenth and sixteenth centuries, when it first blossomed as a genre, was because it was a form of escape from the terrible wars that ravaged the country at the time. For samurai in the era of constant war, linked verse was like the tea ceremony; it allowed one to escape, if only for a brief time, from the world at large, from all the bloodshed. The joy of it was that one could do that in the close company of friends and companions. When the verse sequence was over, one came back to earth, to reality. The same occurred in the tea ceremony as developed by Sen no Rikyū. The tea hut took one away from the cares of this world, together with one's friends and companions.

In short, linked verse, both orthodox linked verse (renga) and its comic or casual version (haikai), was fundamentally imaginary. The *hokku*, or opening verse of the haikai sequence, which later became haiku, required a seasonal word, which marked the time and place of the gathering, but it too had no restrictions with regard to the question of fiction. Indeed, poets often composed on fixed topics (*dai*), which were established in advance. Buson, one of the great poets of haiku of the late eighteenth century, was in fact very much of a studio or desk poet. He composed his poetry at home, in his study, and he often wrote about other worlds, particularly the tenth and eleventh century Heian aristocratic world and the subsequent medieval period. One of his most famous historical poems is *Tobadono e gorokki isogu nowaki kana,* probably composed in 1776. (All translations are my own.)

> to Toba Palace
> five or six horsemen hurry—
> autumn tempest

Toba Palace, which immediately sets this in the Heian or early medieval period, was an imperial villa that the Cloistered Emperor Shirakawa (1053-1129) constructed near Kyoto in the eleventh century and that subsequently became the location of a number of political and military conspiracies. The galloping horsemen are probably warriors on some emergency mission—a sense of turmoil and urgency embodied in the season word of autumn tempest (*nowaki*). An American equivalent might be something like the Confederate cavalry at Gettysburg during the Civil War or the militia at Lexington during the American revolution. The *hokku* creates a powerful atmosphere and a larger sense of narrative, like a scene from a medieval military epic or from a picture scroll.

Another noted historical poem is Buson's *Komabu-ne no yorade sugiyuku kasumi kana,* composed in 1777.

> the Korean ship,
> not stopping, passes
> back into the mist

Komabune were the large Korean ships that sailed to Japan during the ancient period, bringing cargo and precious goods from the continent, a practice that had long since been discontinued by Buson's time. The Korean ship, which is offshore, appears to heading for the port but then gradually disappears into the mist (*kasumi*), a seasonal word for spring and one associated with dream-like atmosphere. The Korean ship passing into the spring mist creates a sense of mystery, of a romantic other, making the viewer wonder if this scene is nothing but a dream.

Another example from Buson is *inazuma ya nami moteyueru akitsushima,* composed in 1776.

> lightning—
> girdled by waves
> the islands of Japan

In this hokku, the light from the lightning (*inazuma*), a seasonal word for autumn associated in the ancient period with the rice harvest (*ina*), enables the viewer to see the waves surrounding all the islands of Akitsushima (an ancient name for Japan that originally meant the islands where rice grows richly). This is not the result of direct experience. It is a spectacular aerial view—a kind of paean to the fertility and beauty of the country—that would only be possible from far above the earth.

Even the personal poems can be imaginary. A good example from Buson is *mi ni shimu ya naki tsuma no kushi o neya ni fumu* (1777).

> chill sinking deep—
> stepping on my dead wife's comb
> in the bedroom

The opening phrase, *mini ni shimu* (literally, to penetrate the body), is an autumn phrase that suggests the chill and sense of loneliness that sinks into the body with the arrival of the autumn cold and that here also functions as a metaphor of the poetís feelings following the death of his wife. The poem generates a novelistic scene of the widower, some time after his wife's funeral, accidentally stepping on a comb in the autumn dark, as he is about to go to bed alone. The standard interpretation is that the snapping of the comb in the bedroom brings back memories of their relationship and has erotic overtones. But this is not about direct or personal experience. The fact is that Buson (1706-83) composed this while his wife was alive. Indeed Buson's wife Tómo outlived him by 31 years.

Why then the constant emphasis by North American haiku poets on direct personal experience? The answer to this is historically complex, but it should be noted that the haikai that preceded Bashō was almost entirely imaginary or fictional haikai. Much of it was so imaginary that it was absurd, and as a result it was criticized by some as "nonsense" haikai. A typical example is the following hokku found in *Indōshū* (*Teaching collection*, 1684), a Danrin school haikai handbook: *mine no hana no nami ni ashika kujira o oyogase.*

> making sea lions and whales
> swim in the cherry blossom waves
> at the hill top

The hokku links cherry blossoms, which was closely associated with waves and hill tops in classical Japanese poetry, to sea lions and whales, two non-classical, vernacular words, thereby comically deconstructing the poetic cliché of "waves of cherry blossoms." Bashō was one of the critics of this kind of "nonsense" haikai. He believed that haikai should describe the world "as it is." He was in fact part of a larger movement that was a throwback to earlier orthodox linked verse or renga. However, to describe the world as it is did not mean denying fiction. Fiction can be very realistic and even more real than life itself. For Bashō, it was necessary to experience everyday life, to travel, to expose oneself to the world as much as possible, so that the poet could reveal the world as it was. But it could also be fictional, something born of the imagination. In fact, you had to use your imagination to compose haikai, since it was very much about the ability to move from one world to another. Bashō himself often rewrote his own poetry: he would change the gender, the place, the time, the situation. The only thing that mattered was the effectiveness of the poetry, not whether it was faithful to the original experience.

One of the chief reasons for the emphasis in modern Japan on direct personal observation was Masaoka Shiki (1867-1902), the late nineteenth century pioneer of modern haiku, who stressed the sketch (*shasei*) based on direct observation of the subject as the key to the composition of modern haiku. This led to the ginkō, the trips to places to compose haiku. Shiki denounced linked verse as an intellectual game and saw the haiku as an expression of the individual. In this regard Shiki was deeply influenced by Western notions of literature and poetry; first, that literature should be realistic, and second, that literature should be an expression of the individual. By contrast, haikai as Bashō had known it had been largely imaginary, and had been a communal activity, the product of group composition or exchange. Shiki condemned traditional haikai on both counts. Even if Shiki had not existed, the effect would have been similar since Western influence on Japan from the late 19th century has been massive. Early American and British pioneers of English-language haiku—such as Basil Chamberlain, Harold Henderson, R. H. Blyth—had limited interest in modern Japanese haiku, but they shared many of Shiki's assumptions. The influence of Ezra Pound and the (Anglo-American) Modernist poetry movement was also significant in shaping modern notions of haiku. In short, what many North

American haiku poets have thought to be uniquely Japanese had in fact its roots in Western literary thought.

We are often told, particularly by the pioneers of English language haiku (such as D.T. Suzuki, Alan Watts, and the Beats) who mistakenly emphasized Zen Buddhism in Japanese haiku, that haiku should be about the "here and now." This is an extension of the notion that haiku must derive from direct observation and personal experience. Haiku is extremely short, and therefore it can concentrate on only a few details. It is thus suitable for focusing on the here and now. But there is no reason why these moments have to be only in the present, contemporary world or why haiku can't deal with other kinds of time. This noted haiku appears in Bashō's Narrow Road: *samidare no furinokoshite ya hikaridō.*

> Have the summer rains
> come and gone, sparing
> the Hall of Light?

The summer rains (*samidare*) refers both to the rains falling now and to past summer rains, which have spared the Hall of Light over the centuries. Perhaps Bashō's most famous poem in *Narrow Road* is *natsukusa ya tsuwamonodomo ga yume no ato* in which the "dreams" and the "summer grasses" are both those of the contemporary poet and of the warriors of the distant past.

> Summer grasses—
> traces of dreams
> of ancient warriors

As we can see from these examples, haiku moments can occur in the distant past or in distant, imaginary places. In fact, one of Buson's great accomplishments was his ability to create other worlds.

Bashō traveled to explore the present, the contemporary world, to meet new poets, and to compose linked verse together. Equally important, travel was a means of entering into the past, of meeting the spirits of the dead, of experiencing what his poetic and spiritual predecessors had experienced. In other words, there were two key axes: one horizontal, the present, the contemporary world; and the other vertical, leading back into the past, to history, to other poems. As I have shown in my book *Traces of Dreams: Landscape, Cultural Memory, and the Poetry of Bashō*, Bashō believed that the poet had to work along both axes. To work only in the present would result in poetry that was fleeting. To work just in the past, on the other hand, would be to fall out of touch with the fundamental nature of haikai, which was rooted in the everyday world. Haikai was, by definition, anti-traditional, anti-classical, anti-establishment, but that did not mean that it rejected the past. Rather, it depended on the past and on earlier texts and associations for its richness.

If Bashō and Buson were to look at North American haiku today, they would see the horizontal axis, the focus on the present, on the contemporary world, but they would probably feel that the vertical axis, the movement across time, was largely missing. There is no problem with the English language haiku handbooks that stress personal experience. They should. This is a good way to practice, and it is an effective and simple way of getting many people involved in haiku. I believe, as Bashō did, that direct experience and direct observation is absolutely critical; it is the base from which we must work and which allows us to mature into interesting poets.

However, as the examples of Bashō and Buson suggest, it should not dictate either the direction or value of haiku. It is the beginning, not the end. Those haiku that are fictional or imaginary are just as valid as those that are based on personal experience. I would in fact urge the composition of what might be called historical haiku or science fiction haiku.

Haiku as Non-metaphorical

Another rule of North American haiku that Bashō would probably find discomforting is the idea that haiku eschews metaphor and allegory. North American haiku handbooks and magazines stress that haiku should be concrete, that it should be about the thing itself. The poet does not use one object or idea to describe another, using A to understand B, as in simile or metaphor; instead, the poet concentrates on the object itself. Allegory, in which a set of signs or symbols draw a parallel between one world and the next, is equally shunned. All three of these techniques—metaphor, simile, and allegory—are generally considered to be taboo in English-language haiku, and beginners are taught not to use them.

However, many of Bashō's haiku use metaphor and allegory, and in fact this is probably one of the most important aspects of his poetry. In Bashō's time, one of the most important functions of the hokku, or opening verse, which was customarily composed by the guest, was to greet the host of the session or party. The *hokku* had to include a seasonal word, to indicate the time, but it also had to compliment the host. This was often done allegorically or symbolically, by describing some aspect of nature, which implicitly represented the host. A good example is: *shiragiku no me ni tatete miru chiri mo nashi:*

> gazing intently
> at the white chrysanthemums
> not a speck of dust

Here Bashō is complimenting the host (Sonome), represented by the white chrysanthemums, by stressing the flower's and, by implication, Sonome's purity. Another example is *botan shibe fukaku wakeizuru hachi no nagori kana*, which appears in Bashō's travel diary *Skeleton in the Fields* (*Nozarashi kikō*).

> Having stayed once more at the residence of Master Tōyō, I was about to leave for the Eastern Provinces.

> from deep within
> the peony pistils—withdrawing
> regretfully the bee

In this parting poem the bee represents Bashō and the peony pistils the host (Master Tōyō). The bee leaves the flower only with the greatest reluctance, thus expressing the visitor's deep gratitude to the host. This form of symbolism or simple allegory was standard for poets at this time, as it was for the entire poetic tradition. In classical Japanese poetry, objects of nature inevitably serve as symbols or signs for specific individuals or situations in the human world, and Japanese haikai is no exception. Furthermore, poets like Bashō and Buson repeatedly used the same images (such as the rose for Buson or the beggar for Bashō) to create complex metaphors and symbols.

It is no doubt a good idea for the beginner to avoid overt metaphor or allegory or symbolism, but this should not be the rule for more advanced poets. In fact, I think this rule prevents many good poets from becoming great poets. Without the use of metaphor, allegory, and symbolism, haiku will have a hard time achieving the complexity and depth necessary to reach mainstream poetry audiences and to become the object of serious study and commentary. The fundamental difference between the use of metaphor in haiku and that in other poetry is that in haiku it tends to be extremely subtle and indirect, to the point of not being readily apparent. The metaphor in good haiku is often buried deep within the poem. For example, the seasonal word in Japanese haiku tends often to be inherently metaphorical, since it bears very specific literary and cultural associations, but the first and foremost function of the seasonal word is descriptive, leaving the metaphorical dimension implied.

Allusion, Poetry about Poetry

The emphasis on the "haiku moment" in North American haiku has meant that most of the poetry does not have another major characteristic of Japanese haikai and haiku: its allusive character, the ability of the poem to speak to other literary or poetic texts. I believe that it was Shelley who said that poetry is ultimately about poetry. Great poets are constantly in dialogue with each other. This was particularly true of haikai, which began as a parodic form, by twisting the associations and conventions of classical literature and poetry.

One of Bashō's innovations was that he went beyond parody and used literary and historical allusions as a means of elevating haikai, which had hitherto been considered a low form of amusement. Many of Bashō and Buson's haikai in fact depend for their depth on reference or allusion to earlier poetry, from either the Japanese tradition or the Chinese tradition. For example, one of Buson's best known hokku (1742) is *yanagi chiri shimizu kare ishi tokoro dokoro.*

fallen willow leaves—
the clear stream gone dry,
stones here and there

The hokku is a description of a natural scene, of "here and now," but it is simultaneously an allusion to and a haikai variation on a famous waka, or classical poem, by Saigyō (1118-1190), a 12th century poet: *michinobe ni shimizu nagaruru yanagi kage shibashi tote koso tachitomaritsure* (*Shinkokinshū*, Summer, No. 262).

by the side of the road
alongside a stream of clear water
in the shade of a willow tree
I paused for what I thought
would be just a moment

Bashō (1644-94) had earlier written the following poem (*ta ichimai uete tachisaru yanagi kana*) in *Narrow Road to the Interior* (*Oku no hosomichi*), in which the traveler (Bashō), having come to the place where Saigyō had written this poem, relives those emotions: Bashō pauses beneath the same willow tree and before he knows it, a whole field of rice has been planted.

a whole field of
rice seedlings planted—I part
from the willow

In contrast to Bashō's poem, which recaptures the past, Buson's poem is about loss and the irrevocable passage of time, about the contrast between the situation now, in autumn, when the stream has dried up and the willow leaves have fallen, and the past, in the summer, when the clear stream beckoned to Saigyō and the willow tree gave him shelter from the hot summer sun. Like many of Bashō and Buson's poems, the poem is both about the present

150

and the past, about the landscape and about other poems and poetic associations.

The point here is that much of Japanese poetry works off the vertical axis mentioned earlier. There are a few, rare example of this in English haiku. I give one example, by Bernard Eibond, a New York poet who recently passed away, which alludes to Bashō's famous frog poem: *furuike ya kawazu tobikomu mizu no oto* (an old pond, a frog jumps in, the sound of water).

> frog pond . . .
> a leaf falls in
> without a sound

This haiku deservedly won the Japan Airlines First Prize, in which there were something like 40,000 entries. This poem has a haikai quality that Bashō would have admired. In typical haikai fashion, it operates on two fundamental levels. On the scenic level, the horizontal axis, it is a description of a scene from nature, it captures the sense of quiet, eremetic loneliness that is characteristic of Bashō's poetry. On the vertical axis, it is an allusive variation, a haikai twist on Bashō's famous frog poem, wittily replacing the frog with the leaf and the sound of the frog jumping in with no sound. Einbond's haiku has a sense of immediacy, but at the same time it speaks to the past; it enters into dialogue with Bashō's poem. In other words, this haiku goes beyond the "haiku moment," beyond the here and now, to speak across time. To compose such haiku is difficult. But it is the kind of poetry that can break into the mainstream and can become part of a poetic heritage.

The vertical axis does not always have to be a connection to another poem. It can be what I call cultural memory, a larger body of associations that the larger community can identify with. It could be about a past crisis (such as the Vietnam War or the loss of a leader) that the poet or a community is trying to come to terms with. The key here is the larger frame, the larger body of associations that carries from one generation to the next and that goes beyond the here and now, beyond the so-called haiku moment. The key point is that for the horizontal (contemporary) axis to survive, to transcend time and place, it needs at some point to cross the vertical (historical) axis; the present moment has to engage with the past or with a broader sense of time and community (such as family, national, or literary history).

Nature and Seasonal Words

One of the major differences between English-language haiku and Japanese haiku is the use of the seasonal word (*kigo*). There are two formal requirements of the hokku, now called haiku: the cutting word, which cuts the 17 syllable hokku in two, and the seasonal word. English-language haiku poets do not use cutting words *per se*, but they use the equivalent, either in the punctuation (such as a dash), with nouns, or syntax. The effect is very similar to the cutting word, and there have been many good poems that depend on the cutting. However, there is no equivalent to the seasonal word. In fact, the use of a seasonal word is not a formal requirement in English-language haiku, as it is for most of Japanese haiku.

In Japan, the seasonal word triggers a series of cultural associations which have been developed, refined, and carefully transmitted for over a thousand years and which are preserved, transformed, and passed on from generation to generation through seasonal handbooks, which remain in wide use today. In Bashō's day, seasonal words stood in the shape of a huge pyramid. At the top were the big five, which had been at the core of classical poetry (the 31-syllable waka): the cuckoo (*hototogisu*) for summer, the cherry blossoms for spring, the snow for winter, the bright autumn leaves and the moon for autumn. Spreading out from this narrow peak were the other topics from classical poetry—spring rain (*harusame*), orange blossoms (*hanatachibana*), bush warbler (*uguisu*), willow tree (*yanagi*), etc. Occupying the base and the widest area were the vernacular seasonal words that had been added recently by haikai poets. In contrast to the elegant images at the top of the pyramid, the seasonal words at the bottom were taken from everyday, contemporary, commoner life. Examples from spring include dandelion (*tanpopo*), garlic (*ninniku*), horseradish (*wasabi*), and cat's love (*neko no koi*).

From as early as the eleventh century, the poet of classical poetry was expected to compose on the poetic essence (*hon'i*) of a set topic. The poetic essence was the established associations at the core of the seasonal word. In the case of the warbler (*uguisu*), for example, the poet had to compose on the warbler in regard to the arrival and departure of spring, about the emergence of the warbler from the mountain glen, or about the relationship of the warbler to the plum blossoms. This poetic essence, the cluster of associations at the core of the seasonal topic, was thought to represent the culmination and experience of generations of poets over many years. By composing on the poetic essence, the poet could partake of this communal experience, inherit it, and carry it on. (This phenomenon is true of most of the traditional arts. The beginner must first learn the fundamental forms, or *kata*, which represent the accumulated experience of generations of previous masters.) Poets studied Japanese classics such as *The Tale of Genji* and the *Kokinsh¤*, the first imperial anthology of Japanese waka poetry, because these texts were thought to preserve the poetic essence of nature and the seasons as well as of famous places.

Famous places (*meisho*) in Japanese poetry have a function similar to the seasonal word. Each famous place in Japanese poetry had a core of poetic associations on which the poet was obliged to compose. *Tatsutagawa* (Tatsuta River), for example, meant *momiji*, or bright autumn leaves. Poets such as Saigyō and Bashō traveled to famous poetic places—such as Tatsutagawa, Yoshino, Matsushima, Shirakawa—in order to partake of this communal experience, to be inspired by poetic places that had been the fountainhead of the great poems of the past. These famous poetic places provided an opportunity to commune across time with earlier poets. Like seasonal words, famous places functioned as a direct pipe to the communal poetic body. By contrast, there are very few, if any places, in North America that have a core of established poetic associations of the kind found in famous places in Japan. And accordingly there are relatively few English haiku on noted places.

The point here is that the seasonal word, like the famous place name in Japanese poetry, anchors the poem in not only some aspect of nature but in the vertical axis, in a larger communal body of poetic and cultural associations. The seasonal word allows something that is small to gain a life of its own. The seasonal word, like the famous place name, also links the poem to other poems. In fact, each Japanese haiku is in effect part of one gigantic, seasonal poem.

People have often wondered about the brevity of the Japanese poem. The seventeen syllable haiku is the shortest form in world literature, and the thirty-one syllable waka or tanka, as it is called today, is probably the second shortest. How then is it possible for poetry to be so short and yet still be poetry? How can there be complexity or high value in such a simple, brief form? First, the brevity and overt simplicity allow everyone to participate, making it a communal, social medium. Second, the poem can be short and still complex since it is actually part of a larger, more complex, poetic body. When the poet takes up one of the topics at the top of the seasonal pyramid or visits a famous poetic place, he or she enters into an imaginary world that he or she shares with the audience and that connects to the dead, the ancients. To compose on the poetic essence of a topic is, as we saw, to participate in the larger accumulated experience of past poets. It is for this reason that the audience takes pleasure in very subtle variations on familiar themes.

This communal body, the vertical axis, however, is in constant need of infusion, of new life. The haikai poet needs the horizontal axis to seek out the new experience, new language, new topics, new poetic partners. The seasonal pyramid can be seen as concentric circles of a tree trunk, with the classical topics at the center, followed by classical linked verse topics, then haikai topics, and finally modern haiku words on the periphery. The innermost circles bear the longest history and are essentially fictional worlds and the least likely to change. The outer circles, by contrast, are rooted in everyday life and in the contemporary, ever-changing world. Many of those on the circumference will come and go, never to be seen again. Without the constant addition of new rings, however, the tree will die or turn into a fossil. One of the ideals that Bashō espoused toward the end of his life was that of the "unchanging and the ever-changing" (fueki ryūkō). The "unchanging" implied the need to seek the "truth of poetic art" (fūga no makoto), particularly in the poetic and spiritual tradition, to engage in the vertical axis, while the "ever changing" referred to the need for constant change and renewal, the source of which was

155

ultimately to be found in everyday life, in the horizontal axis.

Significantly, the Haiku Society of America definition of haiku does not mention the seasonal word, which would be mandatory in Japan for most schools. Maybe half of existing English-language haiku have seasonal words or some sense of the season, and even when the haiku do have a seasonal word they usually do not serve the function that they do in Japanese haiku. The reason for this is that the connotations of seasonal words differ greatly from region to region in North America, not to mention other parts of the world, and generally are not tied to specific literary or cultural associations that would be immediately recognized by the reader. In Japan, by contrast, for hundreds of years, the seasonal words have served as a crucial bridge between the poem and the tradition. English-language haiku therefore has to depend on other dimensions of haiku for its life.

In short, while haiku in English is inspired by Japanese haiku, it can not and should not try to duplicate the rules of Japanese haiku because of significant differences in language, culture, and history. A definition of English-language haiku Japanese haiku will thus, by nature, differ from that of Japanese haiku. If pressed to give a definition of English-language haiku that would encompass the points that I have made here, I would say, echoing the spirit of Bashō's own poetry, that haiku in English is a short poem, usually written in one to three lines, that seeks out new and revealing perspectives on the human and physical condition, focusing on the immediate physical world around us, particularly that of nature, and on the workings of the human imagination, memory, literature and history. There are already a number of fine North American haiku poets working within this frame so this definition is intended both to encourage an existing trend and to affirm new space that goes beyond existing definitions of haiku.

Senryū and English-Language Haiku

Maybe close to half of English-language haiku, including many of the best ones, are in fact a form of senryū, seventeen syllable poems that do not require a seasonal word and that focus on human condition and social circumstances, often in a humorous or satirical fashion. I think that this is fine. English-language haiku should not try to imitate Japanese haiku, since it is working under very different circumstances. It must have a life and evolution of its own.

Senryū, as it evolved in Japan in the latter half of the eighteenth century, when it blossomed into an independent form, was heavily satirical, poking fun at contemporary manners and human foibles. English-language haiku magazines have established a distinction between the two forms, of haiku and senryū, in which those poems associated with nature are placed in the haiku category and those with non-natural subjects in the senryū category. According to the Haiku Society of America, haiku is the "essence of a movement keenly perceived in which nature is linked to human nature." Senryū, by contrast, is "primarily concerned with human nature; often humorous or satiric." While this definition for English language senryū is appropriate, that for English language haiku, which tends, by nature, to overlap with senryū, seems too limited.

One consequence of a narrower definition of haiku is that English language anthologies of haiku are overwhelmingly set in country or natural settings even though ninety percent of the haiku poets actually live in urban environments. To exaggerate the situation, North American haiku poets are given the alternative of either writing serious poetry on nature (defined as haiku) or of writing humorous poetry on non-nature topics (defined as senryū). This would seem to discourage haiku poets from writing serious poetry on the immediate urban environment or broader social issues. Topics such as subways, commuter driving, movie theaters, shopping malls, etc., while falling outside of the traditional notion of nature, in fact provide some of the richest sources for modern haiku, as much recent English-language haiku has revealed, and should be considered part of nature in the broadest sense.

For this reason that I am now editing a volume of New York or urban haiku, which, according to the narrow definition of haiku, would often be discouraged or disqualified but which, in my mind, represents the original spirit of Japanese haikai in focusing on the immediate physical environment. Projects such as Dee Evetts's "Haiku on 42nd Street," in which he presented urban haiku on empty movie theater marquees on Times Square, are, in this regard, both innovative and inspiring.

Conclusion: Some Characteristics of Haikai

The dilemma is this: on the one hand, the great attraction of haiku is its democracy, its ability to reach out, to be available to everyone. There is no poetry like haiku when it comes to this. Haiku has a special meaning and function for everyone. It can be a form of therapy. It can be a way to tap into oneís psyche. Haiku can do all these things. And it can do these things because it is short, because the rules are simple, because it can focus on the moment.

However, if haiku is to rise to the level of serious poetry, literature that is widely respected and admired, that is taught and studied, commentated on, that can have impact on other non-haiku poets, then it must have a complexity that gives it depth and that allows it to both focus on and rise above the specific moment or time. Bashō, Buson, and other masters achieved this through various forms of textual density, including metaphor, allegory, symbolism, and allusion, as well as through the constant search for new topics. For North American poets, for whom the seasonal word cannot function in the fashion that it did for these Japanese masters, this becomes a more pressing issue, with the need to explore not only metaphorical and symbolic possibilities but new areas—such as history, urban life, social ills, death and war, cyberspace. Haiku need not and should not be confined to a narrow definition of nature poetry, particularly since the ground rules are completely different from those in Japan.

How then can haiku achieve that goal in the space of seventeen syllables? The answer is that it does not necessarily have to. One of the assumptions that Bashō and others had about the *hokku* (haiku) was that it was unfinished. The hokku was only the beginning of a dialogue; it had to be answered by the reader or another poet or painter. Haikai in its most fundamental form, as linked verse, is about linking one verse to another, one person to another. Haikai is also about exchange, about sending and answering, greeting and bidding farewell, about celebrating and mourning. Haikai was also about mutual composition, about completing or complementing the work of others, adding poetry and calligraphy to someoneís painting, adding a prose passage to a friendís poem, etc.

One consequence is that haikai and the hokku in particular is often best appreciated and read as part of a sequence, as part of an essay, a poetry collection, a diary or travel narrative, all forms that reveal the process of exchange, linkage, and that give haikai and haiku a larger context. Bashō's best work was *Narrow Road to the Interior (Oku no hosomichi)*, in which the haiku was embedded in a larger prose narrative and was part of a larger chain of texts.

In Bashō's day, haikai was two things: 1) performance and social act, and 2) literary text. As a social act, as an elegant form of conversation, haikai had to be easily accessible; it had to be spontaneous; it had to perform social and religious functions. Thus, half of Bashō's *hokku* were greetings, parting poems, poetic prayers. They served very specific functions and were anchored in a specific place and time, in a dialogic exchange with other individuals. For Bashō, however, haikai was also a literary text that had to transcend time and place, be understood by those who were not at the place of composition. To achieve this goal, Bashō repeatedly rewrote his poetry, made it fictional, gave it new settings, added layers of meaning, emphasized the vertical axis (linking it to history and other literary texts), so that the poem would have an impact beyond its original circumstances. One hopes that more North American haiku poets can take inspiration from this complex work.

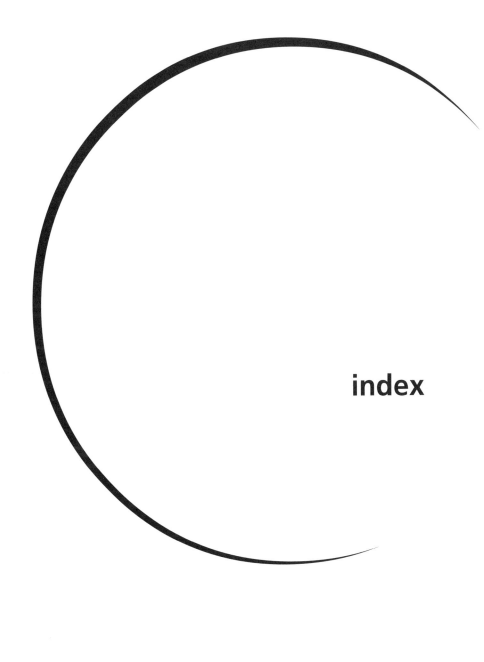

index

index of authors

acknowledgments

Abuza—"heat wave" *Frogpond* XXIII:2; **Addiss**—"birthday snow" *Frogpond* XXIII:2; **an'ya**—"night of stars" *Heron's Nest* II:2; **Anakiev**—"cowbell" *Ginyu* 5; **Aoyagi**—"pre-surgery dinner" *Modern Haiku* XXXI:1; **Beary**—"custody hearing" "all day long" "waiting room" *Pocket Change*; **Berry**—"old garden shed" *Haiku Headlines* 12:10 "no man's land" *162 Haiku*; **Bird**—"spring rain" *Paper Wasp* 6:4; **Board**—"safe for a while" *Five o'clock Shadow*; **Boldman**—"sultry night" "the mourners gone" *Modern Haiku* XXXI:1; **Brandi**—"Fallen leaves" *Stone Garland*; **Brooks**—"mountain butterfly" *Modern Haiku* XXXI:2; **Brophy**—"out of kindness now" *Famous Reporter* 21; **Brydges-Jones**—"my forgetfulness" New Zealand Poetry Society Contest; **Buckley**—"Behind the hearse" *Presence* 12; **Burgess**—"hip fracture" *Pocket Change*; **Cadnum**—"By sunset" *Frogpond* XXIII:1; **Chad**—"in the dark hallway" *tapping the tank*; **Chang**—"new in town" Henderson Contest "Rain" *Frogpond* XXIII:3; **Childs**—"psychology exam" *Frogpond* XXIII:3; "my wife's breast" "first chemo" *Beyond the Paper Lanterns*; **Clark**—"hall mirror & I" *Paper Wasp* 6:4; **Connor**—"Old broom" *Modern Haiku* XXXI:x; **Crook**—"summer solstice" Cricket; **Davidson**—"rain on the skylight" *South by Southeast* 6:3; **Day**—"a salamander" *Frogpond* XXIII:2; **Deming**—"breaking the silence" "one year becomes another" "a leaf falls" *Pocket Change*; **Doderovic**—"Fallen magnolia petals" *Acorn* 4; **Dolphy**—"on a park bench" *Haiku Quarterly* #23/24; **Donegan**—"pampas grass" *The Haiku Calendar 2000*; **Donovan**—"watching the girl" *Pocket Change*; **Doughty**—"peeing after sex" *Frogpond* XXIII:2; **Dunphy**—"All Soul's Day" *Frogpond* XXIII:1; **Duppenthaler**—"into twilight" *Azami* 2000; **Dutton**—"the stillness when rain" *Hummingbird* X:2 "The Bottom Line" *American Haibun & Haiga Volume 1*; **Egger**—"sudden downpour" *Presence* 12; **Eldridge**—"ebb tide" *Wind Bells*; **J.Evans**—"summer thunder" *Frogpond* XXIII:1; **M.Evans**—"midnight snow" *Circled Sunshine*; **Evetts**—"deep in the mountains" *Five o'clock Shadow* "The Conscious Eye: Homelessness" *Frogpond* XXIII:3 "Potatoes" *American Haibun & Haiga Volume 1*; **Falkman**—"Construction & Distortion" *Frogpond* XXIII:1&2; **Fessler**—"beating a rug" *Modern Haiku* XXXI:1; **Ford**—"rainy afternoon" *Haiku Canada Newsletter* XIII:2; **Forrester**—"temple bell ringing" *Modern Haiku* XXXI:2; **Frank**—"haibun" *American Haibun & Haiga Volume 1*; **Fraticelli**—"last night of holidays" *Haiku Canada Newsletter* XIII:2 "Only Words" *Frogpond* XXIII:1; **Gallagher**—"winter drizzle" *Modern Haiku* XXXI:2; "winking" *Raw NerVZ* VI:1 "the closer we get" *Blithe Spirit* 10:2; **Galmitz**—"Behind the wide load" *Frogpond* XXIII:2; **George**—"Winter morning" *Frogpond* XXIII:2; **J.Gilbert**—"leftover drumsticks" *Frogpond* XXIII:1; **R.Gilbert**—"Universalism v. Particularism" HASEE website; **Gilliland**—"morning glory" *Heron's Nest* II:3; **Gorman**—"a child's" "in a field I knew" *Haiku Spirit* 19; "her clingy skirt" *Raw NerVZ* VI:1; **Greenwell**—"geese in flight" *Acorn* 4; **Gurga**—"what to do?" *a penny face up*; **Hall**—"fluttering faster" *Frogpond* XXIII:1; **Hardenbrook**—"the clerk's lip ring" Brady Contest; "mountain hike" Henderson Contest; **Heinrich**—"end of summer" Henderson Contest; **Herold**—"foghorns" Henderson Contest; "just a trickle" *Frogpond* XXIII:1; **Hewitt**—"solar eclipse" *Blithe Spirit* 9:4; **houck, jr.**—"breakfast" *Raw NerVZ* VI:1; **Hoyt**—"drawing the bow" *Modern Haiku* XXXI:3; **Hymas**—"from hand to hand" *Mariposa* 2; **Jensen**—"Waxing Moon" *Frogpond* XXIII:2; **Jones**—"Well thumbed public map" *Presence* 19; **Kacian**—"in concert" *In Concert*; "a time travel novel" *Raw NerVZ* VI:1; "undressing in the dark" *Pocket Change* "Beyond Kigo" *Acorn Supplement* 1; **Kervern**—"Coiled" *Haiku International* 40; **Ketchek**—"gentle snow" *Modern Haiku* XXXI:2; "late snow" *Frogpond* XXIII:2; **Kilbride**—"condolence letter" *Frogpond* XXIII:1 "Losing Private Sutherland" *Frogpond* XXIII:1; **Kimmel**—"surprise visit" *Modern Haiku* XXXI:3; **Klontz**—"overcast" *Haiku Canada Newsletter* 13:2 "Standby" *Frogpond* XXIII:1 "Knotholes" *Frogpond* XXIII:3; **Krivcher**—"train whistle" *Fallen Leaves*; **Lambert**—"Bottles click" *Haiku International* 40; **Lent**—"spring grass" *Acorn* 4; **Lucas**—"new millennium" *Frogpond* XXIII:2; **Lyles**—"into the night" *Mayfly* 28; **Mair**—"night fishing" *Hobo* 24; **Major**—"Adjoining beds" *Modern Haiku* XXX:3; **Makito**—"snake hunting" *Frogpond* XXIII:2; **Matsuzaki**—"first ice over the pond" *Rose Mallow* 39; **McAdoo**—"Breastless" *Frogpond* XXIII:2; **McClintock**—"that kid" *Modern Haiku* XXXI:3; **Mena**—"starless night" Cricket; **Mihajovic**—"After the rain" *Ko* 2000 Spring/Summer; **Mill**—"cold rain" *Frogpond* XXIII:2; **Missias**—"spring morning" *Modern Haiku* XXX:3 "thinking about a man" *Frogpond* XXIII:3; **Monaco**—"Thinking Twice" *Mariposa* 2; **Morrall**—"dark river" *WinterSpin* 2000; **Nakata**—"New rice is boiled" *Haiku International* 40; **Natsuishi**—"Common Ground" *Ginyu* 6; **Ness**—"winter dawn" *Acorn* 4; **Noyes**—"spring morning" *Paper Wasp* 6:4; **O'Connor**—"4 a.m." *Haiku Spirit* 19; **Olson**—"Full moon" Brady Contest; **Owen**—"flea market" *Frogpond* XXIII:3 "pet store" *Frogpond* XXIII:2 "lifting the hammer" *Mayfly* 30; **Painting**—"a dry leaf" *Modern Haiku* XXXI:3; **Pak**—"dark night" *Haiku Moment* 5; **Paulson**—"bedtime story" *Frogpond* XXIII:2; **Pavic**—"going nowhere" *A Scarecrow in the Snow*; **Payne**—"fireflies" *Frogpond* XXIII:2; **Porad**—"long night" *Modern Haiku* XXXI:1; **Payne**—"fireflies" *Frogpond* XXIII:2; **Ramsey**—"Inheritance" *American Haibun & Haiga Volume 1*; **Rohrig**—"Only Words" *Frogpond* XXIII:1 "Waxing Moon" *Frogpond* XXIII:2; **Rollins**—"this long journey" *Presence* 12; **Russell**—"the dog sings" "March Rain" *Haiku Calendar 2000*; **Sari**—"airport strike" *Modern Haiku* XXXI:1 "on thewrong platform" *Frogpond* XXIII:2 "a waning moon" *Famous Reporter* 24; **Scanzello**—"tonight's lecture" *Frogpond* XXIII:3; **Schwerin**—"The mortician" *Modern Haiku* XXXI:3; **Shelton**—"creaking pew" *Frogpond* XXIII:2; **Sherman**—"lilacs by the bridge" *Modern Haiku* XXXI:3; **Shigemoto**—"firefly" *Frogpond* XXIII:2; **Shirane**—"Beyond the Haiku Moment" *Modern Haiku* XXXI:1; **Simin**—"Waiting" *Haiku International* 40; **Spence**—"country road" *Seasons of the Year*; **Spiess**—"the pines on shore sway" Christmas Card 1999:2; **Stefanac**—"gingko biloba" Hawai'i Education Contest; **Steinberg**—"cenetery wind" *Frogpond* XXIII:2; **Stevenson**—"homeless man" *Modern Haiku* XXXI:1; "snow" *Frogpond* XXIII:2; "early Alzheimer's" *Geppo* XXII:6; **Story**—"Thinking Twice" *Mariposa* 2; **Stuart-Powles**—"winter solstice" *Haiku Headlines* 12:9; **Swede**—"intensive care" *Frogpond* XXIII:3; **Tarquinio**—"sectioned oak" "chest to chest" *Frogpond* XXIII:1 "winter night" *Frogpond* XXIII:2; **Tasnier**—"standing up" *Time Haiku* 12 "lengthening winter" *Acorn* 4 "pledging eternal love" *Modern Haiku* XXXI:3; **Taylor**—"abandoned cabin" *Frogpond* XXIII:3; **Thompson**—"house guests" *Pocket Change*; **Tico**—"autumn evening" Henderson Contest; **Trumbull**—"click of the shutter" *Acorn* 4; **van**

den Heuvel—"city street" *Five o'clock Shadow*; **Vayman**—"fortress wall" *Haiku Moment*; **Verhart**—"tin soldiers" *Frogpond* XXIII:1 "Knotholes" *Frogpond* XXIII:3; **Vermeeren**—"storm clouds gather" *Rose Mallow* 39; **Vest**—"thoughts of youth" *Frogpond* XXIII:1; **von Sturmer**—"each day less light" *Frogpond* XXIII:2; **Watsky**—"cafeteria" *Frogpond* XXIII:1; **Welch**—"meteor shower" Henderson Contest; "Valentine's Day" Brady Contest; **Wicker**—"rain and more rain" *Heron's Nest* II:6; **Witata**— "A hot barrel" *Mainichi Daily News* Contest; **Witkin**—"twilight" *Acorn* 4; "another ballgame" *Pocket Change*; **Yarrow**—"backstroke" *Frogpond* XXIII:3; **Zackowitz**—"fresh snow" *Frogpond* XXIII:2 "scattered thoughts" "north wind" Cricket "Standby" *Frogpond* XXIII:1; **Zuk**—"The Milky Way" *Modern Haiku* XXX:3

CITED SOURCES

Books:

a penny face up, Lee Gurga (tel-let press, Charleston IL, 2000). $5US
A Scarecrow in the Snow, Aleksandar Pavic (Moment Books, Novi Sad Yugoslavia, 2000). NP
Beyond the Paper Lanterns, Cyril Childs (Paper Lantern Press, Lower Hutt New Zealand, 2000) $10NZ
crinkled sunshine. ed. D. Claire Gallagher (Haiku Society of America, New York, 2000). $9US
Fallen Leaves, ed. John Thompson (Two Autumns Press, San Francisco CA, 2000). $6US
Five o'clock Shadow, ed. Dee Evetts (Spring Street Haiku Group, New York NY, 2000). *$5US*
In Concert, Jim Kacian (Saki Press, Normal IL, 2000). $5US
Pocket Change, ed. Ellen Compton *et. al.* (towpath haiku society, Washington DC, 2000). $5US
Seasons of the Year, Alan Spence (pocketbooks, Edinburgh Scotland, 2000). NP
Stone Garland: a haiku journey: northern Viet Nam, (Tooth of Time Press, Corrales NM, 2000). $10US
tapping the tank, (ed. Vivienne Jepsen, New Zealand Poetry Society, Wellington, 2000). $19.95NZ
The Haiku Calendar, ed. John Barlow (Snapshot Press, Liverpool England, 1999). $9.95US

Periodicals:

Acorn (ed. A. C. Missias, 436 Spruce St. #2, Philadelphia PA 19106 USA)
Albatross (ed. Ion Codrescu, Str. Soveja No. 25, Bl. V2, sc. B, ap. 31, 8700 Constanta, Romania)
ant ant ant ant ant (ed. chris gordon, PO Box 16177, Oakland CA 94610 USA)
Azami (ed. Ikkoku Santo, c/o Santcel, CPO Box 361, Osaka 530-91 Japan)
black bough (ed. Charles Easter, 188 Grove Street #1, Somerville NJ 08876 USA)
Blithe Spirit (ed. Caroline Gourlay, Hill House Farm, Knighton, Powys LD7 1NA Great Britain)
Famous Reporter (ed. Lyn Reeves, 51 Proctors Road, Dynnyrne, Tasmania 7005 Australia)
Frogpond (ed. Jim Kacian, PO Box 2461, Winchester VA 22604-1661 USA)
Geppo Haiku Journal (ed. Jean Hale, 20711 Garden Place Court, Cupertino CA 95014 USA)
Ginyu (ed. Ban'ya Natsuishi, 3-16-11 Tsuruse-Nishi, Fujimi, Saitama, 354-0026 Japan)
Haiku Canada Newsletter (ed. LeRoy Gorman, 51 Graham West, Napanee, Ontario K7R 2J6 Canada)
Haiku Headlines (ed. David Priebe, 1347 W. 71st Street, Los Angeles CA 90044 USA)
Haiku International (Haiku International Assoc., 9-1-7-914 Akasaka, Minato-ku, Tokyo 107 Japan)
Heron's Nest (ed. Christopher Herold, 816 Taft St., Port Townsend WA 98368 USA)
Haiku Moment (ed. Zoran Doderovic, 21000 Novi Sad, Sumadijska 20, Yugoslavia)
Haiku Spirit (ed. Sean O'Connor, 32 Thornville Avenue, Kilbarrack, Dublin 5 Ireland)
Hobo (ed. Janice Bostok, Campbell's Road, Dungay NSW 2484 Australia)
Hummingbird (ed. Phyllis Walsh, PO Box 96, Richland Center WI 53581 USA)
Ko (ed. Koko Kato, 1-36-7, Ishida-cho, Mizuho-ku, Nagoya, 467-0067 Japan)
Mainichi Daily News (ed. Kazuo Sato, 1-1-1 Hitotsubashi, 1-chome, Chiyoda-ku, Tokyo 100-51 Japan)
Mariposa (ed. D. Claire Gallagher, 848 Elmira Drive, Sunnyvale CA 94087-1229 USA)
Mayfly (ed. Randy Brooks, 4634 Hale Drive, Decatur IL 62526 USA)
Modern Haiku (ed. Robert Spiess, PO Box 1752, Madison WI 53701 USA)
Paper Wasp (ed. John Knight *et. al.*, 7 Bellevue Terrace, St. Lucia, Queensland 4067, Australia)
Penumbra (ed. John Flood, PO Box 940, Manotick, Ontario K4M 1A8 Canada)
Presence (ed. Martin Lucas, 12 Grovehall Avenue, Leeds LS11 7EX, England, UK)
Raw NervZ (ed. Dorothy Howard, 67 Court Street, Aylmer (QC) J9H 4M1 Canada)
Rose Mallow (ed. Yoko Sugawa)
South by Southeast (ed. Josh Hockensmith., RC Box 93, 28 Westhampton Way, Richmond VA 23173 USA)
Sparrow (ed. Marijan Cekolj, Smerovisce 24, 10430 Samobor Croatia)
Spin (ed. various, 7 Megan Avenue, Pakuranga, Auckland New Zealand)
Still (ed. ai li, 49 England's Lane, London NW3 4YD England)

Contests:

The Gerald Brady Senryu Contest (Haiku Society of America)
The Harold G. Henderson Haiku Contest (Haiku Society of America)
The James W. Hackett Haiku Competition (British Haiku Society)
The Hawai'i Education Association Haiku Contest
Mainichi Daily News Yearly Haiku Contest
New Zealand Poetry Society Contest

On-Line Sources:

Cricket
Haiku News
HASEE Website
Shiki Internet Haiku Salon

The RMA Editorial Staff

Jim Kacian (1996-2000) is a co-founder of the World Haiku Association, editor of *Frogpond*, and owner of Red Moon Press.

Dimitar Anakiev (2000) is a co-founder of the World Haiku Association, and recipient of the Medal of Franz Kafka in 2000.

Jan Bostok (1996-2000) has recently, in partnership with John Bird, set up HAIKUOZ: The Australian Haiku Society on the net.

Tom Clausen (1996-2000) works in a library at Cornell University and lives with his family in the house where he grew up.

Ellen Compton (1996-2000) is a freelance writer with a background in visual and theatre arts, and a deep love for the earth.

Dee Evetts (1996-2000) is a carpenter in New York City by day, and by night the moderator of the Spring Street Haiku Group.

Maureen Gorman (1997-2000) believes her study of haiku is a perfect complement to her work as a professional counselor.

Kohjin Sakamoto (1997-2000) is a university professor who has written haiku in English as well as Japanese for over two decades.

Alan Summers (2000) began writing in Queensland; now in Bristol, U.K., he's immersed in the myriad possibilities of haiku.

George Swede's (2000) latest books are *Almost Unseen* and *Global Haiku* (as editor with Randy Brooks).

Jeff Witkin (1996-2000) has published two books of haiku and tanka. As best he can, he lives each moment as did Seymour Glass.

RMA Editors-Emeritus: **Lee Gurga** (1998), **Yvonne Hardenbrook** (1996-8), **John Hudak** (1996-7), **H. F. Noyes** (1996-9), **Francine Porad** (1996), **Ebba Story** (1996).

The RMA Process

DURING THE TWELVE MONTH PERIOD December 1, 1999 through November 30, 2000, over 1600 haiku and related works by over 1000 different authors have been nominated for inclusion in *a glimpse of red: The Red Moon Anthology 2000* by our staff of 11 editors from hundreds of sources from around the world. These sources are, in the main, the many haiku books and journals published in English, as well as the internet. Each editor is assigned a list of books and journals, but is free to nominate any work, from any source, s/he feels is of exceptional skill. In addition, the editor-in-chief is responsible for reading all of these sources, which ensures every possible source is examined by at least two nominating persons.

Editors may neither nominate nor vote for their own work.

Contest winners, runners-up and honorable mentions are automatically nominated.

When the nominating period concludes, all haiku and related works which receive nomination are placed (anonymously) on a roster. The roster is then sent to each of the judges, who votes for those works s/he considers worthy of inclusion. At least 5 votes (of the 10 judges, or 50%—the editor-in-chief does not have a vote at this stage) are necessary for inclusion in the volume. The work of editors must also receive at least 5 votes from the other 9 editors (55%) to merit inclusion.

The editor-in-chief then compiles these works, seeks permissions to reprint, and assembles them into the final anthology.